Zen Jiu Jitsu

White to Blue:

From Confused White to Competent Blue Belt

Oliver S. Staark

This book is for educational and training purposes. The publisher and authors of this instructional book are not responsible in any manner whatsoever fir any adverse affects rising directly or indirectly as a result of the information provided herein. If not practiced safely and with caution, martial arts can be dangerous to you and others. It is important to consult with a professional martial arts instructor before beginning training. It is also very important to consult with a physician prior to training due to the intense and strenuous nature of the techniques in this manual.

All rights reserved. No part of this publication can be
reproduced or transmitted in any form or by any means, electronic or mechanical, without permission in writing from Oliver Staark.

All rights reserved. No part of this book may be used or reproduced in any form whatsoever without written permission except in the case of brief quotations embodied in critical articles or reviews.

ISBN-13: 978-1491023747

ISBN-10: 1491023740

First Edition

Copyright © 2013 Oliver S Staark
All rights reserved.

http://jiujitsubuddha.com

CONTENTS

Foreword
How to Use this Manual
Choosing the Right School
Core Principles
Technique Concepts
Tactical Considerations
Maps and Systems
In Conclusion
Resources and Reference

ACKNOWLEDGMENTS

I would like to thank my professors, coaches and training partners. They remain an inspiration and make the joy of learning jiu jitsu a true gift.

Cover image courtesy of iStockphoto.com

FOREWORD

"I am a shark. The floor is my ocean and most people don't know how to swim."
~ Rickson Gracie - Vale Tudo and BJJ Legend

As a white belt this may come as a surprise, but I'm envious of your position. I'm sure the opposite is true. I remember that time when I was a white belt and would walk into the academy and see those higher belts lining up for the advanced class, they seemed to exist in some rarified atmosphere. Sometimes I would hang around after the fundamentals class and watch the more advanced students roll, they seemed to be doing stuff I couldn't even comprehend. They were the cool kids, submitting each other, laughing it off, discussing something that was a little more technical. I had no clue what was going on for the most part. Enthusiasm was all I had.

This might sound familiar dependent upon the stage you are at right now. So why am I envious?

You are at the entrance to a wondrous forest that is open to exploration. To you this is virgin soil it is an amazing feeling to stand at those gates. When you have been rolling for many years, things change. They are still great but that feeling of learning something basic that clicks and blows your mind gets less and less. The more advanced a student a becomes the more he concerns himself with developing a particular game, this usually comes from experience and many hours of mat time.

Towards the end of his Blue Belt a fighter is aware of how his body type, flexibility, strength, cardio fitness within a particular guard game, this then forms the foundation for the later belts. According to my own professor it's at Black Belt that the next real true learning curve begins, this is where it all comes together and everything starts again. Can't wait.

As a White Belt you need to remember one thing: All black belts stood where you are standing right now. They all began as a White

Belt and moved through the ranks just like you are about to. This is a journey that is not to be rushed, it's a journey to be savored and contemplated. Will there be times when you get frustrated? Sure. Will there be injuries along the way? Sure, what sport can you become excellent at that won't incur an injury or two along the way. Will you feel like giving up after a particularly horrible practice? I'm sure you are reading this and going 'Not me!' well you might think that now, but once that Blue Belt gets tied around your waist, look back and there might have been one or two nights you were ready to throw in the towel.

Like I said at the beginning of this section, I am envious. You are about to be given a gift that few people have the ability to appreciate and enjoy. My heart and mind encourages you to stay on this path. Believe me, you won't regret it.

Best Wishes. Oss.

HOW TO USE THIS MANUAL

"Knowledge grows with time, work and dedicated effort. It cannot come by any other means."
~ Ed Parker - Father of Modern Kempo Karate

Just like the previous text (Zen and the Art of Jiu Jitsu) this is a conceptual manual. Don't expect techniques, this is purely to help you understand and get better with the concepts of Brazilian Jiu Jitsu from White Belt to Blue Belt.

So if you are a Purple Belt you might think, "Huh? This is all obvious information". Yes, it may be obvious after five years plus of training but if you are only six months (or six weeks) into this art form then this information can accelerate your understanding so much that it could put you light years ahead of your teammates.

One of the most frustrating areas of Jiu Jitsu when I started was I didn't know how to put it all together. By the time I had decided to do this jiu jitsu thing and joined in a regular class, the curriculum (the positions being instructed at that time) was on say 'side control' but I had only just learned what the closed guard was. By the time closed guard training came back around in the rotation I had forgotten everything about the closed guard and had to start again.

Also, high school wrestlers were giving me a beating and I just could not figure out why. This book explains the 'Why'. You need to understand core concepts that your professor would love to explain to you but probably doesn't have the time in a fundamental sixty-minute class. He's demonstrating the core techniques, and you should stay present and in the zone when he is demonstrating these techniques. Especially The Details! I'll say that again: Especially The Details!

Once you have the physical side of the core principles in place you need to understand the reason 'Why' you are doing it that way. This not only makes the techniques easier to remember but actually helps you attain the goal faster, even if it's not using the traditional method taught by your coach or professor.

This manual is the 'brain' side of Jiu Jitsu. If you are looking for techniques and refreshers on moves in your curriculum then this isn't for you. Please seek out the various excellent Manuals, Apps, DVD's and YouTube videos that can help.

Towards the end of the book is a section that covers some miscellaneous elements that could still affect the way you train. I've called this area Tactical Considerations, if they do crop up you'll know why I named it that.

The first section is Core Principles. These are concepts that I use to this day and make explaining how important these elements are very easy. If you get nothing else from this program then please read and re-read the Core Principles. You won't regret it. Just note that some times you may also disagree with my interpretation of a Principle. This is natural if that happens. Once you get to Blue Belt please come back and read them again... this time I bet you agree with me at least on some level.

The next section covers Technique Concepts. Like I mentioned earlier, this is not a technique demonstration manual. There are very few images in this volume, but the understanding of 'Why' you are doing what you are doing in side-control, closed-guard, attacking, defending is as important as the moves themselves. Once these concepts are understood and absorbed your game will take on a new dimension. Do not skate over the Technique principles contained within, it's taken me years to understand and distill them so you can easily understand what this whole ball of wax is all about.

Another question I get is: Why concepts? Why not show techniques? Because concepts will take you further than any single technique, they are like principles, they will last you your entire BJJ career.

Finally, the last section has some ideas on where to start if you are struggling trying to get ahead of (or in line with) your academy's curriculum. This is a plan that should give you a firm foundation in the principle techniques of BJJ. It doesn't show the techniques or moves but demonstrates a 'chain-link' plan that if you follow it methodically will give you a great understanding and foundation of the basics of Jiu Jitsu. Keep drilling these techniques and you will become a solid Blue Belt - 100% guarantee with that. Please Note:

This is not intended to replace your own academies curriculum; it is intended to support your practice and training of BJJ.

If you feel your academy does not have any structure at White Belt level and this bothers you then you seriously need to consider training at another academy. Enough said on that subject.

CHOOSING THE RIGHT SCHOOL

Although in the last section I said 'Enough Said on that Subject' I thought I may as well expand - just a little.

When it comes to the academy you train at then many factors will decide on how you arrived there. It could be you knew what you were looking for and tried several academies in your area arriving at one that felt the best, or you enjoyed the most.

Could be a friend, family member or colleague invited you to train with them. This is very common, and is more than likely the highest percentage of how jiu jitsu schools get most of their students - referral.

Also, if there is no introduction made, another common denominator is principal location. This is the strategy used by a lot of health and fitness centers across the world, they place their buildings where it's easy to get to. It appears that people don't want to drive past one fitness center to get to another across town. So the health clubs set up on busy streets and the membership grows. The same is true (to a degree) of BJJ academies; a lot of students join the one nearest to where they live. There is nothing wrong with this by the way, that's how I started.

The best method though in my opinion is to look around at local schools and try them out. Most schools offer an intro lesson, this should be taken advantage of. Watch how the new white belts integrate with each other, ask about cost and how often you can train as part of the white belt program. Some schools are very limited whereas some are available seven days a week, make sure you know and it fits with your schedule regarding the various aspects of your life. If you get the bug then you'll be spending a lot of time there.

Once you've decided and you are working well with the school, then this becomes more of a 'team' issue. I discuss training at different academies in Zen and the Art of Jiu Jitsu. I won't expand here as it's not that important, you need to work closely with your coaches and professors at the academy of your choice. Integrating into the school you have selected needs to be your primary goal.

If you are feeling: small, slightly alienated, intimidated due to your skill level, embarrassed about training with complete strangers or even made to feel slightly unwelcome then check this link: http://breakingmuscle.com/martial-arts/surviving-socially-beginner-phase-bjj

This is a great blog post by Valerie Worthington who really struggled to integrate socially with her academy at the beginning of her BJJ Journey. It's worth a read even if you get along with everyone at your school.

Don't think that the level of instruction at your school will make you into the next Rodolfo Viera or Buchecha, it won't. Only years of dedication and hard work can do that - with a generous helping of talent.

I see students leave our academy from time to time and find them training across town. They use excuses (as far as I can see) that the instruction level wasn't up to the standard they expected. That's fine, expectations vary, but you need to be realistic when it comes to the level of instruction you will receive: some schools are less adept at coaching than others, some are more structured than others, some very competition oriented, some self defense oriented. These various styles may suit what you need or may not. If the school doesn't emphasize the style you need, then switch schools. It's much easier at the white belt level than when you are years into being part of a particular team.

If competition training and success is what you are looking for from your BJJ academy then that should be apparent fairly quickly. If the professor or head coach doesn't have a proven track record of competition success, or if the school doesn't contain a lot of successful competitors then chances are this is not the school for you, seek one out that does have a group of hungry competition oriented students. This way you'll get what you need.

CORE PRINCIPLES

THE TAP
"Cry in the Dojo. Laugh on the Battlefield."
~ Unknown - But Makes Perfect Sense.

There is one thing that makes Brazilian Jiu Jitsu unique compared to other martial arts and that is the Tap or Tap-Out. I don't want to get into any MMA or branding issues about the use of the word TapOut so we'll refer to it here as the Tap.
When you find yourself in a position that you feel (if you continued) may cause you harm then the simple tap-tap on your partners arm, anywhere on his body, the mat or even a verbal tab (sometimes required when you are bent into a position that makes a hand or foot tap impossible) the match or sparring session stops. This is used mostly in sparring and is the greatest advantage over any other martial art.
And what an advantage...
This gives all BJJ practitioners the opportunity to spar full contact, going hard and still not hurting each other. How many other contact sports can boast such a claim. The Tap is the most powerful element in Jiu Jitsu and should not be considered a weakness, as my own professor tells me, "You have to tap a thousand times before you can consider yourself a black belt." He actually uses the mechanism of tapping to keep score of his level of improvement.
Only last week I was rolling with a very good black belt. I was a lot heavier and moved myself into a dominant position. He was telling me not to be so nice and get moving into the submission position. Heeding his words I moved and after a long (and patient) process I eventually managed a tap. When we reset he fixed his Gi and asked me why I was being so nice. I sort of shrugged, I didn't have an answer, maybe I am too nice, maybe I am too respectful of higher ranking belts. Who knows? This is when he hit me with the thunderbolt that made a great connection. "You cannot hurt me. All I need to do is tap." And he tapped me twice on the shoulder to

prove his point. This was him giving me permission to go on the attack. In this sport whether you are attacking or defending you are learning something. It does not benefit you or your partner to go easy, unless it's a light roll by mutual consent or there is a huge disparity in weight, age or rank.

Don't imagine that because a new white belt on his third class at the academy knows how to tap then he's open season. That's not why we're here. But if you put the newbie in pressure positions and help him to look for escapes while trying to submit, then you BOTH improve. If you get in a tough spot with a higher ranking belt or heavier opponent know this: There is no disgrace in tapping.

In fact, if you are just rolling with a buddy (same, weight, age and rank) and he catches you with a clean arm lock and you tap. How do you feel? Do you want to go kick the dog? Scream obscenities at him/her? Or are you proud that your buddy is coming along?

If it's kick the dog or scream then I fear your days as a long term BJJ fighter are truly numbered. This is part of the game and I'm super happy when one of my training partners catches me. If it keeps happening every session then I would talk to my professor or coach for an appropriate escape and the survival options. We'll talk more about those in a later section.

This is one of the reasons that Royce Gracie proved BJJ to be so effective in the original UFC 1. Don't forget this was a very different version of the UFC than what is represented today. This was when it was a game of styles, so Karate would go against Boxing, or Taekwondo against Sumo. Weights and ages etc. were of no consequence, it was all about styles. So little one hundred and seventy five pound Royce would be put against two hundred and fifty pound beasts. And not just for three rounds, this was as long as it took and then after each round he would fight a different opponent until there was one winner. It was true gladiator style back then - bloody and brutal.

Royce though had a secret weapon though…the tap.

He had been training full on sparring all his life. He used leverage to his advantage in real life situations and no-holds-barred matches. The other styles didn't have this capability. Think about it, how could a boxer, taekwondo fighter, muay thai guy or karate stylist go 100 % each sparring session without getting brain damage?

Even if they were strikers that went hard they were always padded up to some degree with gloves, headgear, body armor so when the time came to go all out against an opponent then it was a different experience. They could not spar for real.

Not so for Royce. He had been rolling in the Gi and tapping (and being tapped) since he was kid. He went into the Octagon pulled these poor unsuspecting souls to the canvas and submitted them, to him it was just playing around. This is all seems so matter-of-fact today, but before the world had become exposed to Jiu Jitsu no one had ever seen anything like this.

At the time, this must have been a shocking realization for a lot of the other styles who believed that they were the deadliest men on the planet. The original line-up (and many others in years to come) would tell anyone who would listen that they were real bad-asses. Then they hit Royce Gracie and came up short.

This wasn't achieved because Jiu Jitsu had some secret techniques passed down from Shaolin Monks in a remote Tibetan cave. It was all because Royce could train full contact <u>all the time</u>, and that was only because of the tap.

CREATING THE TRAINING HABIT

"A body at rest tends to stay at rest whereas a body in motion tends to stay in motion."
~ Sir Isaac Newton - Very Smart Physicist

I agree with Sir Isaac here. If you don't get into some kind of routine to keep you in motion then the hypnotic lure of the Tube will break your will. It just about kills everyone's dreams of being good at anything.

Just like any organized training protocol there will come a time when you either:

- Just don't feel like it tonight

- Are looking for excuses to get out of training

- Feel tempted to sit and watch American Idol (or some other mind numbing tripe)

- Clash with another new Sport/Hobby/Pastime

- Feel like doing something else

This malady tends to apply to any kind of fitness program or anything connected with the improvement of the abdominal muscles. Diet programs fall under this umbrella too and BJJ Training is no different.

When it comes time to engage in training you have to have some kind of failsafe in place to make sure you get there. You must have heard the saying "A black belt is a white belt that didn't quit!" You understand that it means actually 'training' on the mat and not just being a BJJ 'member' of the school? You've got to go.

This is an important distinction. I'm sure you will see these guys at your school - don't become one of them. They show up every now and then, sometimes just enough to get a stripe promotion. Usually get to the stage of blue belt and then just trickle along. They wear the tee-shirts, the tattoos declaring their commitment to Jiu Jitsu but they don't seem to train a lot. You'll see them at tournaments and this is where they declare: They got an injury and get can't back into it, they are busy at work/home, they will be back full time next week, they love it.

This is talking...not training. The only way and I mean the ONLY way to get good at Jiu Jitsu is to train. I don't mean you need to be at the academy all the time but you will need to work out with your partners, work on techniques, drill the moves, roll on the mats, spar, etc.

You will notice that during any discussion on the subject of Jiu Jitsu advancement the wearing of a really cool Shoyoroll* tee-shirt is not a pre-requisite.

To a certain degree everyone goes through this stage in some form. When you start to feel like this please understand it is natural. The longer you leave it though, the harder it gets to recover from this condition, and it is a condition. Look at the following statements:

"I'll just have one more slice of cheesecake. Back to healthy eating tomorrow."

"One more Bud won't hurt, I'll be fine for rolling tomorrow morning."

"Shoes off. I'll grab an hour of TV. No need to roll tonight, it's been a long day."

"Watch that Tornado guard DVD later. Real Housewives is on in twenty minutes."

None of these 'excuses' are bad, none of them are life and death decisions. They all relate to time and the time is usually short, it's an hour here and there, or a day at most because then you'll be back on track, right?

That must be the biggest reason that virtually all Home Gym equipment is on Craig's List. The inner voice who I refer to as the 'Terminator' is very powerful. If you need somewhere to hang clothes by the way use the closet, it's a better idea than a piece of home gym equipment.

The reason that I use the expression the Terminator is because it gives a face to that inner voice. It's the devil on my shoulder. He doesn't care if I'm tired, had a long day, need to keep in shape, his only objective is to stop me achieving anything...literally ANYTHING.

The Terminator would have me sit in front of the TV and spoil like old cabbage if it could. But I won't allow that…here's my solution.

On training days, I DO NOT think about training in the evening. I ignore it like I am not even going, as if I don't even do Jiu Jitsu. If I start wondering what section of the curriculum we will be covering or who might be training tonight, it gives the Terminator an opportunity to chime in. And we don't need anyone chiming in thanks.

I don't eat before training or at least three hours before. I don't want to feel heavy or like I'm going to puke when I roll. Furthermore if I do eat late I don't need the Terminator telling me that I will fail because I ate too late. If I know that I am not going to eat until after training there is no play on time to consider whether I should eat or not. My wife knows I'm going to be eating later so she doesn't need to tempt me with anything thirty minutes before I am about to leave. It's a done deal. Terminator squashed at this point.

About one hour before I'm due to leave I take a shower and get into my Gi. This may not be practical for everyone as some guys train straight from work. That's fine, the system works either way, just ignore this paragraph. Take a shower and get in your Gi.

I can hear a question from the back of the room. "What? An HOUR before? Isn't that a little early for getting ready?"

Not especially. First off this is a contact sport. A close contact sport. I'm sure people don't like my B.O. as much as I don't enjoy theirs, so the shower helps keep me fresh. Getting in my Gi alerts my brain that I will be leaving for BJJ any time soon. This keeps the Terminator and any human versions of the Terminator (kids, wife, drinking buddy) from wondering if I fancy just checking out the game. It's a huge visual cue: I am going to train BJJ don't even ask. I'm not stood here in my Karate pajamas because I am ready for bed at 5:30pm. I am going training. Get over it.

Maybe that's the rant I play in my mind when my wife asks me about a drawer that needs fixing. During the hour before I am about to leave, I prepare for Jiu Jitsu, nothing else.

When I say nothing else, I talk to the kids and do homework and all that kind of stuff (in my Gi) without the jacket and a sweatshirt on so I only have short legged pants on display. But I don't do anything that could start up a project and make me late or delay me in any way.

This is my regime, my Training Habit and I do not veer from it. You might come up with a better one, but it has to be a ritual you perform without fail. If there is an opening for failure, guess what, it will fail. I stick to the:

- Not thinking about BJJ until work or my work day is over

- Eating early at least three hours before training time

- Showering

- Getting in my Gi an hour before I leave

This is my Process. And now everyone else is on notice that this is a training day. When I drill techniques at Home in the garage, I don't do any of that. I roll around with the dog pestering me on the mat and neighbors waving as I'm choking my submission dummy.

This process is reserved only for training days. This is how you make sure you stay on the path and keep improving. If you don't need this level of motivation then just keep doing what you're doing and keep improving. If and When you hit a plateau this chapter might come in handy.

The takeaway is this: **You Must Train to Improve. That's it!**

*And Shoyoroll do very COOL tee-shirts and Gi's. Check them out here: http://shoyoroll.com

JIU JITSU WILL MAKE YOU HAPPY

This is another reason to make sure you get to that training session, Jiu Jitsu will make you happy and that's a fact. Researchers and scientists who have been looking into the science of Happiness and have come to the conclusion that the Happiness Hormone is something called Dopamine. Dopamine is technically a neurotransmitter and makes sure the signals in your brain fire at the appropriate times, the more you can get the Dopamine to light your brain up the more happiness we tend to feel.

So what makes the Dopamine get excited and fire up? Well, real happiness isn't the short term smiley feeling we feel when someone buys us something like a gift. That is a more a fleeting bliss or euphoria. This study looks at something more permanent – Long-term Happiness.

The Scientists have realized that to get that Dopamine moving we can do several things:

- Engage in a physical activity that raises the heart rate

- Learn new skills that test us and keep our brain active

- Spend time with friends and family (a sense of community)

Those are the main three that can help us live a long and happy life. Did you notice that all those elements fit perfectly into Brazilian Jiu Jitsu. It's totally cardio-centric, Point (1). We need to keep learning new skills or everyone gets a handle on our game and we get passed, Point (2). The academy is a great place to have a good time and enjoy yourself, Point (3). Even in a tournament environment, once the war is over, all I see are people hugging and shaking hands. It's the safest cure for depression this side of a Prozac infusion.

The Buddhists refer to happiness as inner peace. This is what Jiu Jitsu creates through the testament of the body. Steel sharpens steel.

And what if you can't train. This happens when you get an injury, or are sick or just miss the class due to traffic and you feel bad. It's a genuine low feeling - lack of Dopamine. When this happens (unless I'm sick with flu or some other noxious virus) I still go along to the academy from time to time and check on my teammates. Even that term: Team Mates, makes us close and the BJJ community as a whole could not be closer, I've never engaged in another sport where everyone gets together competes and celebrates. It's unique...and it makes you happy :)

OBSERVATION

"Any Technique, however worthy or desirable, becomes a disease when the mind is obsessed with it."
~ Bruce Lee - Creator of Jeet Kune Do

In Zen Jiu Jitsu I talked extensively about Observation. This covered a lot of ground and if you need to consider this principal with more depth then I suggest you grab that manual too.

The idea of Observation is to keep alert and awake while you are training. If you are fully engaged when you are sparring then you should know (minimum) where all your limbs are. Here we go again, eyes rolling at the back of the room, "But my limbs are there all the time, I know where they are! Left, right, got it."

Next time you spar and find yourself in, say, half guard. I bet you do have some idea where your arms and legs are but I bet they are not active, unless you are just hanging onto your training partner for dear life like a limpet and running the clock down. Whenever you are in a position even side-control or mount where it seems obvious, do a quick body scan. Is everything where it's supposed to be, is it active? If you have a loose hand or arm, or leg then make it tight and get your balance or your grips back in position. This is Observation.

If you are working on a guard position (we'll talk more guard later) then you need to be aware of your feet and grips. Even in closed guard you need to have an awareness. If you don't know why you have your grips in a particular position then you need to clarify that with your coach or professor.

This is one of the most important ideas that I know can help accelerate your progress: Clarity. If something is unclear then don't just press on in an ocean of arms, legs and sweat. Stop, ask your training partner if he can help you. If he can't then ask a coach or your professor after the class is over. Maybe take some private lessons. If you do then make sure you (a) get clarity on any areas that you feel you are lacking, and (b) write it down. In a later section we cover the importance of a training log or training journal but for now a simple notepad will do. Don't misunderstand me here, it's not that you will use the notebook as a reference (you can if you want) but the act of writing things down tends make more of an impression on the mind.

When I think back to my early private lessons I can still remember a lot of the details not because I have a great memory but because I made a lot of notes. Where my hips and grips should be, where my balance should be, good foot or hook positioning.

When you get these details down and someone counters the move easily, you feel a little disheartened. If you are Observing properly though you will soon realize that you had a weak hook, or your grip was on the wrong sleeve leaving an opening. Be vigilant when you train. This is a very important principle to understand, but not at all easy to practice.

USING A TECHNICAL APPROACH

It's worth mentioning that there are specific and general Observation conditions. General Observations are strength and size considerations. We've all heard the Helio stories of the art being developed for 'men with bodies like dead chickens' and this was cool when no one knew what BJJ was. These days, someone steps onto the mat with a college wrestling background and muscles in his spit then you had better have a sound strategy to consider. What if your sparring partner is three hundred pounds? You can see from a general Observation standpoint that you do not want to be on bottom ... unless you're four fifty in which case - you da man!

You cannot get grips unless you lean forward or extend your arms. You cannot launch on top without the use of the legs. These are general trigger points that you should be aware of.

If you are starting on your knees, imagine a line drawn on the mat between you and your opponent horizontally between you, like you are sat in front of a mirror. If your opponent or you cross this line then you can reach (touch) each other. This is the critical distance line (CDL). This is the area of no mans land which tells you a lot about general Observation. You should be able to devise your strategy from here, as soon as a hand or foot crosses that line you need to know what the next move will be ... regardless of whose hand or foot crosses that line.

Specific Observations are the understanding of the attacking units themselves, namely: grips, foot position (which develops the stance) and hips. This is where 95% of your concentration should be focused. If you mentally divide your opponents body down the center as soon as he takes his stance and you monitor his hands he will either get a grip closer to himself (on a pant leg or the collar closest to him) he may go deeper and come for a deep collar or sleeve grip then he will move the second hand. The exception to this would be simultaneous grips, which is rare as most practitioners prefer to get a sense of balance or create tension before latching the next grip.

Each starting attack will have three parts (1) grips, (2) transition, and (3) position. You want to change the path of the attack at the second phase of the transition. This is the easiest way to counter. If you need to change your strategy or have more time - release their grips - no one attacks without some form of grip. If you are attacking first then you will work your protocol, but the process will more than likely be the same: grip, transition, position (and if you've drilled it well enough), submission.

You will need to intercept their transition at the beginning of the phase - certainly not at the end. This can lead to your guard being passed and then you will need another counter. To do this you will need to (a) monitor the baseline of your opponent closely so you can see which side his weight shifts, and (b) install your strategy as soon as he begins his attack. These you can drill once you get into the Zen JJ thirty-day program.

Most students don't even think about the counter until the attack is well on its way. This is a folly. They sleep through the grips and foot positions and don't even realize that an attack is happening until they land in side control or a scramble. Proper Observation and good execution and grip control should cut this down quite a bit.

To make Observation even easier to work with, use the technique known as 'side-tracking'. You form a grip structure or stance you are happy with. Until you get the grips you want, then you break your opponents grips all the time. Next assign a technique that covers any position if your opponent moves to the left, you have a left side counter. If he moves to the right then you have a right side counter (from the stance and grips you have). If he breaks your grip, you have a counter and if he leans backward or forward you have attacks.

Only four techniques to learn: left side, right side, grip break, leaning (forward or backward). There should be no crossover techniques. This will expose quickly if you are awake or not.

I drilled this for a couple of weeks and found that when my opponent moved right I did the left hand technique and was handily passed because I confused myself by being asleep and not drilling enough. It didn't matter though. The fact that I thought about it, saw the move coming and had a strategy made me feel pretty good. Another week later and no one passed the stance I was starting with and I was moving into good positions time after time (and against some pretty tough opponents too).

Most newbie students positions are less than spectacular usually because (1) they went into full-on sparring too soon, (2) they have been taught only technique positions and are unaware of transitions, (3) they have not been taught how to spot an attacking grip, or (4) they have failed to confront and engage the attack.

Now you have a method for creating awareness, spotting an attack and countering. Enough practice and these should become natural movements. Now it just needs the accompanying physical work and the rest will follow.

Creating awareness while sparring, you have to, in this order:

Monitor the attacking units. Concentrate and focus. Mentally move forward with the attack until you recognize what your opponent plans to do. Reaching out and crossing the critical distance line means you are ready to confront and engage your opponent.

- Spot the attack and counter the transition as soon as it begins

- Counter and move into a position of control

- Counter failed, break grips and reset

- Focus intently on the hips at all times, as this is the balance of power and know at all times where your own hips are.

If you are having trouble and still getting suckered from time to time then try this. Monitor the attacking units 100% even when attacking. You will still need to move and pass or submit but keep these areas in your periphery. It's a little weird at first as we are so intent on reaching our target but a few things can happen.

When you are intently focused on the hands and feet of your opponent you are better prepared for counter attacks. After a while just focus on hands and your own hips, you'll find adjustments in range and the pressure easier to handle. The strange phenomenon with this technique is that it helps tremendously with passing the guard, just keep the pass in the periphery and stay focused on the hands, feet and hips and you'll eventually slip by your opponent almost unnoticed.

TIME ON THE MAT

"Great things are possible when one man's wisdom and an hour's effort are combined."
~ Choi Hong Hi - Founder of Taekwondo

Regardless of your motivations to start training in Brazilian Jiu Jitsu, the surest way to improve is spending time on the mat. Mat time is one of the biggest factors that will determine your speed with which you will progress.

When you first start to train and there are no white bars on your belt only that black strip of fabric there will probably be other people stood beside you. They are in the same position or maybe a little more advanced, maybe one white stripe on the black fabric. Now, I want you to imagine that these people (your teammates) are your speedometers on your journey from white to blue.

Look around. I don't mean this to become a competition with your teammates, they are just a reflection of where you are. Right now, you are in what I call the first condition of the learning cycle: You don't even know what you don't know yet. Don't worry that will change, it gets even scarier when you realize actually how much you don't know!

When your teammates turn up to train, check your progress against them. Keep in mind all the other salient factors of being in a contact sport: physical condition, age, weight, etc. There is no point in comparing yourself to a twenty one year old ex-high-school wrestler who weighs two hundred pounds when you are forty, have a wife and two kids and haven't done any kind of physical activity for ten years. But still, keep an eye on the kid. If he is accelerating in pace and you are struggling with concepts, ask his advice. You'll probably find that he is spending more time on the mat than you.

This can also translate into 'be on the mat all the time'. That's not the message. Consistency is the message. Avoiding injuries, learning and most of all enjoying yourself while you are doing it. Time on the mat is an important factor in all of this. But don't become the academy pest who gets injured due to overtraining then can't train for two months.

To keep consistent get a copy of your academies schedule, choose the classes that you would like to train on. These will usually be the most suitable times and classes that fit your rank. So don't think you are ready to jump into the advanced classes when your white belt is new and shiny. Pick the classes where you can learn the basic and the fundamentals the most. Get in good drilling time, improve your conditioning and get a handle on the details in techniques. This would be a perfect class for a white belt.

Now draw a block around each class in red pen and pin it somewhere you will see often. I go one step further and just slot those classes into my online schedule. It beeps my iPhone one hour before class so I know I had better start getting ready.

This beats the inner demon again - The Terminator. You have an appointment to make. This makes the hour or ninety minutes a carved in stone block of time that is not to be missed. If you have other people in your life: wife, kids, girlfriend, boyfriend, etc. Then let them also have a look at the schedule and see if it fits in with everything else you've got on. When I first did this, my wife booked herself in for a fitness boot camp at the same time, so it worked really well. It kept her in line with her fitness goals and it made it easier for me to go train BJJ. No point in sitting around in an empty house waiting for her to get home from boot camp.

My initial training program was just three times per week. I would book in two sessions during the week and one on the weekend. This worked. Then as I improved in technique and my conditioning improved so that I could do specific training for longer (our academy doesn't allow white belts to spar until they have been through the sixteen week fundamental curriculum) I upped my training to four days. Now it's five.

You'll notice I didn't go from three times per week to six days per week. There were some guys that did that. They don't train anymore. Some come back from time to time but then they can't cope with the mental trauma of the guys who started with them (or later) giving them a hard time on the mat. This is BJJ so there are no real smash-sessions but to be easily handled and dominated by someone who is older, more unfit and sporting a knee brace isn't the best for the ego or moral.

That's what consistency breeds. To a degree that is one thing that jiu jitsu has in common with golf. It's the swing, the technique that makes the ball go for miles not the muscle. The way to a great swing is to consistently swing in a great way. It's no secret, for the most part its common sense - use it.

DRILLING

"Practice until you are exhausted…then practice some more."
~ Norman Harris – Sensei

Can you handle two quotes in this section?

"Learning Jiu Jitsu is something for the sub-conscious, not for consciousness."
~ Helio Gracie - Co-Creator of Gracie Jiu Jitsu

This is probably the greatest game changer in this manual. This is the one thing that made all the difference to my game and it will to yours.

Time on the mat sometimes doesn't mean time on the actual mat, it means time working on your Jiu Jitsu and this can be Drilling technique, at the academy or elsewhere. Think carefully about this.

Would you go to a Golf tournament, or even play a round with your friends if you hadn't bothered to hit the driving range first?

How many Tennis players play without hours of practice on the basics?

How many Baseball players don't bother with that pesky batting cage?

How many boxers think the heavy bag is a total waste of time and that they would perform equally as well without it?

How many…

Okay, you get the drift.

But seriously, think about your BJJ training. How much time do you put aside to drill armbars, side-control to mount, triangles…anyone? Yet, we expect to perform like we have been drilling when it comes to specific training or sparring!

Most BJJ Academies don't have time to fit in teaching a technique, drilling it (adequately) and then running through specific training. In a ninety minute training session it would be difficult for your professor or coach to build in a long enough drilling session. Therefore, you must find time to drill technique yourself.

When you complete a fundamentals session with your professor or coach and you get home, spend five to ten minutes on the rug in the lounge covering what you just did. You don't need a training partner just go through the moves. If you are motivated to really build a drilling session into your program then set an hour aside to drill techniques between classes.

Personally, I use several training aids and my garage looks like a small academy. Right now, at the white belt stage I wouldn't encourage you to go that far. Once you feel like you are committed to BJJ, maybe when you hit Blue Belt, then you might want to take the leap. At white belt level just mentally cover the steps to deliver a good armbar, a good triangle, keep the details in place.

It helps to have a focus when you are drilling or it just ends up a bit of a sea of moves but feels like a workout. When I was beginning I even went a step further and completed the same warm up we did at the school before my drilling session. As my body became accustomed to the routine I didn't feel as uncoordinated or gassed as some of my fellow trainees. It showed me right away that drilling paid off.

If you don't have an idea of what to focus on then jump to the Maps and Systems section towards the end of the manual. This will give you some ideas. As you get more organized and your drilling becomes part of your weekly workout, get a white board in the garage and start to add some specific exercise that help with your training.

I have a tight groin and have had several groin strains (super painful) over the years. Now I warm up and then do some specific Ginastica Natural techniques and some physio moves to help with my groin stretches and strengthening.

Here are some suggestions to work on with your drilling program (there are more in the Maps section):

- Attack: Armbar from the closed guard

- Defense: Side Control Escape

- Sweep: Scissor Sweep

- Mount: Cross Choke

- Back: Rear Naked Choke

- Half Guard: Escape from someone's half guard. (I drill this every time I have a drilling session as one of my Go-To moves. This is because landing in half-guard is very common when you train on your knees.)

All of these techniques can be practiced without a partner if you move your hips. The armbar is somewhat difficult as you are raising your hips off the ground and using your partner to swivel and pivot. But the mechanics can be covered. Do these ten times each. It should feel like you have had a mini-workout when you're done. You will have covered the basic moves to get you through a closed guard specific training session. This will give you a massive advantage on your training partners if you only do one hour per week. Just imagine what you can accomplish if you take that up that to two hours per week!!

When you have more experience and want to upgrade your drilling then you should really upgrade to some training aids. There is a section at the back with some recommendations.

GRADIENT LEARNING

THIS IS AN EXCERPT FROM THE ORIGINAL ZEN AND THE ART OF JIU JITSU MANUAL:

Keep forgetting techniques? Not learning to roll as well as you should? Maybe you just don't know what you don't know! This is the first stage: 'unconscious incompetence'.

Below is an adaptation on how we apply the data on learning styles so that it makes sense in a Jiu Jitsu lesson or a drilling session.

To win a match or sparring session then you need to get from Point A (usually a standing or kneeling position) to Point B, this could be a submission or you could break things down further and consider a sweep, pass or move to side control or dominant position as success. This seems straightforward but do you have the links clear in your mind that get you from A to B to C...?

I am going to use an adapted version of the four learning stages for our purposes in Jiu Jitsu. Ignoring the unconscious competence area, as you already know that some part of your game is lacking (or you are a white belt and have no real concept of the techniques yet), we move on to phase one:

1. The Cognitive Phase. This is the process where you see the parts of a technique. Consider the armbar. It takes several steps to get from the closed guard to the armbar as an example:

- Secure the arm

- Place the foot on the hip

- Swivel your own hips to create angle

- Throw leg over face

- Lift hips for tap

This is a (very) simplified version but you get the drift. Most beginners see this process and try to speed through it, this is a mistake. At the cognitive phase the opposite should be true. Slow down. Understand each step, when your professor or coach mentions a detail then concentrate on the detail, this will be important - I guarantee it. Make it slow enough that you understand how the pieces fit together.

This advice applies to all levels. When Marcelo Garcia samples some new position he doesn't just watch it on YouTube then start flying into it in the academy. He will study the chain of events that comprise the technique, link them together in his mind and then drill it possibly adding his own flavor (but he's a genius so don't do the flavor bit when you are drilling a new technique). Which leads us to:

2. The Associative Phase. This is where you can visualize yourself flowing through the entire technique. WITH NO PARTS MISSING. Once you know physically how the pieces fit together stop and see in your mind how that process works. If you can visualize yourself moving through the whole process that means that you understand the technique. If you get brain fog half way through, drill it again - slowly - in steps and realize which part you left out. Once you start rolling you can try the technique and if it doesn't come off check in and see what happened. This is covered in more depth in the section on Observation.

It's important to recognize that some people stop here. They learn the steps, they can see it in their minds, they sample it in sparring - it works. No need for further exploration. They are short changing themselves. They need to continue to:

3. The Autonomous Phase. This is where the stimulus automatically produces response. Let me offer a real world example. One of my favorite stances (starting positions) in sparring is the Butterfly Guard. So I sit with my knees splayed and am very conscious of the distance between myself and my partner. I then hunt for the cross-collar and elbow grip, I can get this most times as it can be very non-threatening to my opponent. Once I'm latched onto my partner he only has a few options available to pass my guard. I have drilled every possible option at least two hundred times.

Doesn't matter to me if they grab my pants at the knee, below the knee, break my grip, posture up, scoot to the right, scoot to the left, push their weight forward. I pretty much have a set piece response.

Now this isn't to say that I cannot be passed or my partner won't have a counter to my attack but I do know that I don't have to think too much so that I can counter his counter if necessary or worry more about the pass if it looks like he has broken my technique.

If an arm is presented I will have an attack for the arm. If my partner slips up in anyway I am pretty much prepared. This was a revelation to me. For the first couple of years I was just rolling around getting very sweaty in the process. Then something clicked, and this only happens after tons of reps and a roadmap of what I should be repping.

Think about it. If you learn to drive stick shift, you know: control the clutch, change gears with your hand, etc. took a driving test and passed. Congrats! Then you put the car away and then three years later you think let's take it for a spin. How do you imagine you would handle the controls? You might pull it off but you've dropped back to the Cognitive Phase. Nice and slow and going through the steps hoping you don't stall it at a traffic signal on the highway.

Now if you've been driving stick for three years every day I bet sometimes you'll arrive at your destination and can't even remember the journey?? That's how automatic your sense of process has been. You are in phase four, the Autonomous Phase. No thought, just action. And this is where we want to aim.

This is much harder to accomplish in the striking arts. For example, how many hooks does a boxer have to slip before it becomes reflex? Probably thousands, so we need to count our blessings that the gentle art does afford us some time to adapt to this process. Things move at a much slower pace in grappling and this should make our drilling efforts much more efficient.

Ultimately it boils down to taking things one step at a time, or gradient learning. The mindset of 'gotta have now' won't work with most proficiencies and Jiu Jitsu is no different. Get to a point where you can just do the move or technique then set about drilling it.

A final note on 'drilling' or 'repping' a technique. Make sure you understand it and that all the various points are in place before you drill. A bodybuilder would not carry out thousands of reps on a body part that was already well developed. And you should not be repping a technique badly.

This is where your road map comes in. Stick to the plan. Rest when you should and keep going forward when you are assigned to do so. Don't start straying off the path, the overall result will be less powerful.

HIP CONTROL

"If nothing within you stays rigid, then outward things will disclose themselves."
~ Bruce Lee - Creator of Jeet Kune Do

I can still hear Chubs, Happy Gilmore's golf coach, telling Happy, "It's all in the hips...it's all in the hips." He was talking about golf of course, but the same applies to Jiu Jitsu. If you don't know who Happy Gilmore is, he is a comedic creation of Adam Sandler. The character who turned from hockey player to golf pro...with laughs of course.

But the "It's all in the hips" line stuck with me. So many sports depend upon the hip yet it's often overlooked. When kids, or even adults, want to demonstrate their athletic prowess they make a bicep or puff out their chest. It's not very common for someone to swing a hula hoop move and say check out how athletic I am. Maybe in the adult movie business? But we're getting off topic.

George Foreman was one of the hardest hitting heavyweights in history. He was renowned for breaking guys ribs with body punches, and when interviewed about how come he hit so hard, what do you reckon his answer was: "It all comes from the hips."

Now in Jiu Jitsu we don't strike or swing a club for that matter but still, the hips are where all the action takes place. To move into any position we need to be in constant communication with the hip, both your own and your opponents.

If you are in a top position with your weight bearing down, you would need to lock your opponents hip. So, if you manage to pass and get into side-control-top then you would concern yourself with locking the hip. Yes, head control is super-important, but locking the hip is the best habit to get into. If you are stuck inside your opponents closed guard, then you must use your knees and grips to lock his hip in position so you can break the guard.

You will often hear in the academy things like 'he has heavy hips.' This is what they are referring to. When someone is on top and they transfer their weight down on you through the hip, it is just a matter of time before gravity does the rest and you are in a tough spot.

Let's look at bottom positions. Your opponent passes and bears his weight down on you, the opposite of the previous scenario. You need to hip escape and then get a knee back in there to prevent him from gaining control again. Don't forget, in a competition setting, passing the guard is not enough, you need to maintain control for three seconds then you get three points for the pass. Don't give up if someone passes, just use your hips and escape.

In closed-guard-bottom, this is a key position for attacks. To attack and have an active guard you need your hips to be free, hence, break the posture of your opponent.

Just like the example of heavy hips above for the top position, consider the bottom position to be a fortress that no one can pass. Using your feet to move your hips or control your posture will create a sturdy enough guard to take your game higher.

A lot of white belts don't think about posture unless they are in a top position. That closed guard samurai kind of seated position, which looks and feels noble. On the bottom though, the white belt thinks attack-attack-attack, which is good. But for now I would like you to think posture, top and bottom. On top, keep your posture good and your hips solid, on bottom break your opponents posture using your legs this will free the hips for the attack.

As Master Carlos Gracie jnr put it, "Your legs are your hips. Take the way a snake moves. It doesn't walk; it zig-zags. Jiu Jitsu fighters playing guard look like snakes [only] with their bellies up." If you are to become proficient in any ground fighting game then you need your hips to be active, and to neutralize your opponent you need to disable his hips so he can't move them.

This is a groundbreaking realization for a white belt to understand. By the time you get to Blue or Purple then this will seem clear, but try to keep your hips on the move and if you pass your opponents guard: Lock those suckers down.

HIP ESCAPE

This is the signature move of a Brazilian Jiu Jitsu player. This is why it is incorporated into our warm ups and most new students look like they are having seizure when trying to understand it. Not a natural move...but an essential move.

In all the techniques I have thought about, considered and become competent with over the years, the hip escape is still something I drill fifty times each day. When I go to my drilling session I lay on my back and hip out twenty-five to each side. Then I pull in the grappling dummy, and hip-out into the scissor sweep position. I don't sweep the dummy just hip out to each side.

This is a pretty good warm up and it prepares the body to move automatically to very defined defensive positions. If it even looks close to someone passing my guard, my body just moves, bam, auto-responsive into a knee shield.

The other day this became clear when one of the professors at my academy was demonstrating a technique and chose me as the demonstration dummy. I lay down and he was pushing me into shape and speaking to the class about each position step along the way. I was listening too as I knew I would be training it with my partner, then he pushed my knee down to pass and my hips scooted out as my knee came in and blocked him. Obviously, this wasn't part of the technique, he laughed and pushed my knee back then said, "You see what happens when you've done a thousand hip escapes." Automation. Unconscious competence.

Not all automation is good as we discussed in the section on Observation, it's good to be awake and aware for the most part and in control of yourself and your opponent. But when it comes to defenses, the pure speed of reaction is what can save you. It would be difficult to see a strike coming in at you full force to the face and your brain say, 'hey, let's duck right'. Too late. Whammo! The right hand clipped you and you're down. That's why boxers spend so much time on slipping drills.

One of the main goals of the hip escape is Guard Replacement and that's where you need to start when a white belt. Don't concern yourself with hip escaping to slide a cool hook inside the thigh of your partner, that can come later, after your guard replacement has become automated.

As a funny little side note, I always get a laugh out of white belt student when I ask them 'how do they know when the hip-escape is truly engrained in the brain?' Most aren't sure or think it's a matter of reps. Not so…it's when you hip escape out of bed, or hip escape to roll over IN bed! Then you know you've truly got the hip-escape in your blood, now it's just on auto-pilot.

TRAINING DIARY

"The way of martial arts starts with 1,000 days of training and is truly commanded after 10,000 days of training."

~ Masutatsu Oyama - Founder of Kyokushin Karate

Ever noticed those guys in the gym that write all their weights and reps down. I used to think they were gym nerds, as though they would go home and plot their weight training progression. And that may have been true...because they were a lot smarter than me!

When I was into weight training, many years ago, I would go and workout at the gym, lifting as heavy as I could for as many reps as I could. It was aimless and I worked out that once I reached a plateau on the weight front I didn't really progress in strength or conditioning for around six months. I was a little frustrated and asked a trainer what I might do to improve and he asked me a couple of questions about my poundages and my sets/reps and the protocol of training I was using. For most of the questions I just shrugged. I didn't have an answer because I couldn't remember the weights/reps or programs I had been using. This made me look like the gym dork, now I wished I were a nerd.

He sort of laughed at me and in a nice way told me to run along until I could answer the questions. I gave up soon after and probably took up some other hobby that didn't require the power to write stuff down.

Today is different. In the gym I workout and record everything in my smart phone. I have an App that tracks my sets, weights and programs and measures results...even has the ability to print charts with my improvements showing and clear plateaus. Pretty cool, please don't tell the nerds.

Now the same is true of your BJJ Training. Grab a small notepad and stick it in your gym bag or leave it at home if you go to the academy changed but as soon as you get home write down the following:

- The Date

- Who the Coach was for the session

- What you learned the most from that lesson

- First Technique

- Second Technique

- Training Partners

- What was the position for Specific Training

- How did Specific Training (or Sparring) go?

- Session start and finish time.

Let me cover the thought process behind these remarks. The date is obvious, the name of the coach too. But I have had coaches that I really enjoyed their class and some coaches I didn't. This was duly noted.

What you learned most. This is a more expansive question and not a mechanical question. The answer is not Guillotine Escape or Triangle. The answer would be something like: I really like side control from the top, I feel real comfortable and have a killer choke that seems to get everyone. That's the correct answer, it's more of a personal feeling than a direct quote from the curriculum.

First and Second Technique. Now you can go to the curriculum. This is a memory jogger. You can even add a detail or two. For example, Don't forget to grab my wrist instead of my fingers when pulling the guillotine into position.

The position for Specific Training. Again, this is pretty much a solid position: side control, mount, closed guard, etc. Writing this down gets you used to the terminology and the positions pretty quickly. Also you will relish some positions and groan when others present themselves. As time wears on you will soon come to relish the positions that cause you problems, trust me.

How did it go? Did you crush your training partners like flies or did you get crushed. Was it a mixed bag? More accurately, what worked and what didn't, especially what didn't. Write it down, you'll need to come back to it. If training went well then writing it down and acknowledging it is a form of positive feedback. It increases your confidence in positions using mental self-talk, sounds a bit 'out there' but it seems to work.

Also make a note of your energy levels. Was it all cool and you felt relaxed? Did you gas out after the first round? Did you have a heavy dinner too close to training? Were you full of energy and could have sparred all night? The notes don't have to be negative, just make a note.

Start time and Finish time. This is worth noting as a pattern can sometimes present itself. When you look back on your notes you might see that you felt better and trained better on certain days of the week and times. This could be related to circadian rhythms or it could be as simple as your body is warmer and more ready for combat at one time as opposed to another. I tried training first thing in the morning for a while and it just did not agree with me. Talking to a doctor he mentioned that some people have a core body temperature that just doesn't get revved up until they have been out of the sack a couple of hours. It appears I suffer from this condition so training times do matter. I just hope no one attacks me first thing in the morning.

And why write all this down? Why not just memorize it? I'm sure you won't be pulling your notebooks out to reminisce with the grandkids anytime soon, but you will commit some things to memory far more effectively than just thinking 'I got that move down' or 'I was on fire tonight'. Keeping your thoughts written down in an organized manner helps keep the filing cabinet of the brain in an orderly fashion. It commits the techniques that matter to memory much better than just 'trying' to remember. An old school teacher of mine used to say 'a short pencil is better than a long memory' and over time I have come to agree with him.

Another item I use to keep a handle on my training commitment is a calendar. I use one of those blotter kind of calendars that sits under my computer keyboard for most of the year and I can make notes and doodles on. Each month has a box to represent each day, this is supposed to be used as some kind of schedule I assume. When the month is over I tear off the page and a new month is revealed.

After each training session, and just before I hit the hay, I just note down the amount of time I trained in the box for that day. It's as simple as 1 HR, which means one hour or 1.5 HR, which is one and a half hours. If something eventful happened I put a little Asterisk * next to the time.

When the end of the month comes around I can see if I put the hours in or if I was a lazy ass. I total up the time and then write that number in the first square if the next month. This is the training time I will not drop below. It's a semi-goal number though I don't check during the month how well I'm doing, I just train.

As for the Asterisk's I check the date then go back to my notebook at the beginning of the new month. This will reveal what happened in that training session and why it was eventful. This might be important in my plan for the next month.

NEGATIVE SPACE

"For the choke, there are no 'tough guys'. With an armlock he can resist the pain. With the choke he just passes out and goes to sleep."
~ Helio Gracie - Co-Creator of Gracie Jiu Jitsu

This is a principal I wish I had been aware of when I began Jiu Jitsu: The concept of Space and Negative Space.

Have you ever thought when you roll with some of your teammates that their game is tight? It seems as if a boa constrictor is wrapped around you somehow, even though they are not muscling you or using strength. This is what negative space means and this is how they are achieving this effect.

Instead of really pulling and pushing your partner around on the mat, or trying to leap over them with some flamboyant move try to imagine that once your grips are in place you will leave no gaps, no holes, for them to move around. You will impose your game on them.

Let's take closed guard bottom as an example. As mentioned in a previous section the idea of the guard is to control the distance between you and your opponent. When they are in your guard, you are in control*, they can only open your guard and pass, or that's what they should be trying to do.

On bottom, you should be thinking attack (that can be a sweep or submission). Now which attack should be choose? Let's go for the cross collar choke, nice and simple to discuss here, but entrenched with details.

You slip your right hand into his right collar (cross collar), adjust until it's deep, fight for the next collar grip. Pull twist, grunt, groan...and still no tap. Why?

Too much space. Think negative space. How can this be achieved?

One word: **Posture**.

To reduce the space (and therefore control the space) you will need to break your opponents posture. I am sure you will have heard your professors or coaches say this many times, but as happened with me you might be thinking 'sure' but how?

They might show you a technique on breaking posture but as soon as you are in an open sparring situation you default right back to trying to sweep the guy, he blocks it and passes and then (sigh) it's all about escaping side control - again!

Let's look at this again from the perspective of Negative Space.

If the guy on top has strong grips and can pin you to the mat immobilizing your hips so he can move his knees into position try this. Get the best grip you can on both his elbows, flare them out while pulling with your own knees toward your chest. The guys arms buckle and he will fall right on top of you. Now get an under-hook (that's getting your arm under his armpit) and pull him further into you. I bet he'll look surprised. It's the sensation of falling forward flat on your face without your arms to protect you from the fall - face plant style. The space is now ... closed.

Go back to the cross choke, slide the right hand in deep. If he starts resetting his grips, use your left hand on his elbow and pull him in with your thighs again. This time as he slides upright, keep the tension down with the right hand grip and using your left pull the collar further down so that hand is DEEP in his collar. If you can feel the thumb joint of your right hand touching the back of his neck, that's deep enough.

Now allow him to erect himself as if going for the posture up again. Slide the left hand underneath and into the collar while controlling him with your thighs. Go deep as you can. The trap is already set by the right hand, then using your whole body to curl inward go for the tap.

Go to YouTube and search "cross collar choke from the guard" I was going to add a link here, but there are so many good examples that you could spend the next hour checking this out. Just keep an eye on the negative space - there is no room (or shouldn't be) the guy on bottom is totally pulling his opponent into a position that is difficult for him to recover. Don't forget, the guy on top has only one goal: to break the guard, his next step would be to pass. If you are on the attack and there is no space to move his hips so that he can't break your guard - he's a sitting duck!

*Believe it or not, the closed guard has a very close resemblance to the mount. This is a VERY dominant position learn to use it well.

SPACE

As the section previously stated, negative space keeps your game tight. It makes everything come together in one element. Ever had that feeling when someone was glued to you; that's negative space.

The opposite is, well, space. And as with all things jiu jitsu there is a vice versa to each concept. When you are on the wrong end of a smash pass, what do you think you need? No, not a Berimbolo slide out, you just need a little space.

Most white belts try to stop the pass with a hand, which is quite correct as this will buy you enough time to create space…and that's where the system fails.

How many times have you moved into side control (or even been on bottom and been guilty of this yourself) and the guy on bottom tries to bench press you away. Not down towards his hips as a release but as in a regular bench press, up in the air, away from his chest. He's just trying to create space just doing it in the wrong direction.

This is especially true when bigger guys get passed by smaller guys. If you're a big guy, don't do this, it's not cool on the little guys and doesn't work on the bigger guys.

Some of you may disagree. That's fine, no need to disagree with me, just disagree with gravity and unless you can bench press two hundred pounds for five minutes continuous, guess what, the bigger guy will pass as your chest and arms fail. Then you a super screwed. No strength to create more space and now you have been passed with possible head and arm control and the other guys shoulder under your chin and stuck in your throat.

It's better to use leverage to create some space so your hips can move. This is what the fundamentals program teaches us, but as a white belt you are probably still using strength and some tension, this is natural. Try and relax on bottom. I know it's hard to do, but your potential to escape will increase dramatically if you go all loosey-goosey on bottom and just slink right out of there.

A lot of sports are determined by the amount of space they create. Most team sports like football, basketball and soccer can be decided on the team that creates the most space for their team to work. This is true of BJJ. If you are in a tight spot and looking to create opportunities, space must be created, this is a path to victory.

So it's a combination, if you are on the attack utilize negative space, if you are on the defense or looking to counter: create space. It's that simple, though not easy, you need to work at it.

BALANCE

"The wise man wins before the fight, the ignorant man fights to win."
~ Morihei Ueshiba - Creator of Aikido

Of course when performing any kind of stand up part of your game, balance is essential. If you have a hankering to experience why this is so then go to a couple of judo classes, you'll soon pick it up. Balance and the distribution of weight through feel (and especially the balls of the feet) is imperative.

Now, Brazilian jiu jitsu is a ground game, so a majority of our time is spent on our back, side, shoulders, even our heads on occasion. How should balance be distributed?

This was a concept I struggled with as a white belt. I felt it was okay to go with the flow, so if someone came in with a sweep I would usually get swept and then start to work from the bottom. I wasn't a very successful or effective white belt, not sure if I mentioned that. This is not a strategy for success, believe me, I really gave it a go but beatings on beatings proved that having an effective base is important.

Again, let's revisit this word: Base. I am sure you will have heard it in class, 'keep a strong base' it's much akin to Posture. One of those words that coach's say and white belts seldom understand, so here's my interpretation to help you better keep your balance and base.

Base, according to the dictionary is:

1. the lowest part or edge of something, esp. the part on which it rests or is supported:

2. a conceptual structure or entity on which something draws or depends:

3. the main place where a person works or stays:

4. a main or important element or ingredient to which other things are added:

5. Chemistry: a substance capable of reacting with an acid to form a salt and water, or (more broadly) of accepting or neutralizing hydrogen ions. Compare with alkali.

6. Electronics: the middle part of a bipolar transistor, separating the emitter from the collector.

7. Linguistics: the root or stem of a word or a derivative.

8. Mathematics: a number used as the basis of a numeration scale.

9. Baseball: one of the four stations that must be reached in turn to score a run.

verb

1. have as the foundation for (something); use as a point from which (something) can develop:

2. situate as the center of operations: (-based)

The best comparative I can glean from this is 'the lowest part or edge of something, esp. The part on which it rests or is supported', I also like 'the main place someone works' but the first is a better comparison for this section. When you kneel in front of your opponent and you touch knuckles, this is what you should be representing: an obelisk, a statue of granite that cannot be moved never mind swept aside.

Try this exercise. When another white belt pulls guard or you are specific training in a closed guard capacity, don't try to break or pass. Just think Base, just think posture and do not allow your training partner to break your posture or disturb your base. You are a rock, molding yourself to the mat, you are made of granite.

Now, this is super frustrating to the guy on bottom as he tries to attack and fails (he needs to break your Posture) or tries to pull a sweep that fails (Base) and for you it gives you a sense that you can do this. You are surviving and safe.

Okay, but say he breaks your posture and sweeps you. Great. You just found something out, you learned that you do not have a good base, or you have a poor posture when in guard. Before you start developing your game - fix this! It's that important.

One time I was working my base and posture with a guy. I spread my knees nice and wide, his legs locked around my waist. My weight slumped down low onto my heels like I had a lead belly, my spine erect, my right arm locked on his collars over his breastbone and my left pushing down on his hip. I was locked in position and I was not going to move. I wanted to see if there was a weakness in my base or posture.

This guy had his girlfriend on the sidelines videoing him, like he was going to kick everyone's ass on the mat and record it for giggles. I just bedded down deep, and he was trying to come at me but he was pinned like a butterfly with a needle through it. He tried and tried and I just locked him down for four minutes then broke his guard and passed. When the coach called Time this guy flipped out, he was calling me all kinds of bullshit moves, I just laughed.

He pulled off his belt and told his chick 'let's go' then they stormed off. She gave me a withering look before she followed him. I call this the walk of shame. If you feel the need to storm off because you've been frustrated while rolling, or just plain beat then shame on you. Don't do it. That's the real bullshit move, not the keeping of a good posture and fine base.

If you decide to stand to break guard then you need to be aware that the number of sweeping options just increased incrementally. Standing to break guard is a great option (the best actually), but keep your base low as soon as you have broken the guard, elbows tucked inside the knees, hips low and feet nice and wide apart. You don't want to get suckered with a double ankle sweep, and I see brown belts getting caught with this on occasion.

Standing is all part of the game. When you are preparing for a tournament you will have to get used to starting standing.

There is a famous jiu jitsu statistic, I'm not sure if it's true or not (and if it is then I'm totally confused how it could have possibly been calculated): Around 80% percent of all street fights end up on the ground. This is valuable data if you are ground fighting specialist but please consider this: 100% of all street fights start standing up.

It's important to start from standing, you need will cover this a little more when you are starting to build your game before blue belt sinks in. Just be aware of your balance if you decide to stand while sparring.

INSIST VS PERSIST

One of the things I used to hear my professor say when I was back in my white belt days was 'insist'. This is an interesting concept to consider as I think he got the terminology wrong even though I hear it over and over from both American and Brazilian coaches.

It's usually used in the context of a scramble. For the purposes of this text we will define a scramble as a neutral position where either opponent could come out on top with neither in a clearly defined position. It's more of a wrestle than a technical display, but it does happen. When two opponents get caught in a scramble then grips will be in odd positions and a single leg might present itself so one of the players grabs it and goes for the single. His opposite number doesn't want to get swept so he posts and lots of shoving and grabbing ensues, usually with a coach on the side screaming 'insist, insist...'

Now, if the guy holding the single keeps pushing he is either going to get the sweep or they are going hit something, like a wall or spectators or other fighters rolling. The guy getting swept who is posting is getting forced back but he is also supporting his weight and pressing back against his opponent. One of them will give up eventually. That's just gravity. Simple physics.

What does the word 'insist' mean in this context? I used to hear it and think I can't insist he fall on his ass because I have a single leg. That's like insisting he let me win, it just wouldn't happen.

This confused me. Until I replaced it in my head with a better word: Persist.

This now meant 'don't give up,' keep going. So if I am sweeping I will be persistent in my manner. As soon as this concept changed and dropped into my brain some of my training partners started noticing that when I got in to a scramble and grabbed something I would not give up, we slammed into walls, steamrolled team mates, fell off the mat onto watching beginners but I would not stop.

If someone thought this wasn't cool, then I just told them to give it up and give me the sweep. They had to make a decision, it worked out best for both training partners if there was persistence and resistance. If everyone were persistent it would become pretty much a matter of conditioning.

Don't get me wrong, I have been on the opposite end of this too. When my partner was 'insisting' he win and I was persisting in pushing back (resisting). Ultimately my muscle failed or my gas tank ran dry and they passed, or swept or got grips, whatever I didn't want to happen happened! But I persisted in keeping the faith and tried not only to win but also to not-lose. I would recommend you do the same.

ATTITUDE

Remember the story I mentioned earlier in the section on balance, and I mentioned the 'walk of shame' that is the epitome of a bad attitude. Don't let the events on the mat change your attitude, and I know how hard this can be. Ready for another tale of woe?

When I was a three stripe white belt I used to train between two academies. They were part of the same association under the same professor but had different members training there as they were in distinct parts of town. My schedule was pretty flexible so I could train at both and this gave me a variety of training partners, which I still enjoy to this day.

While getting involved in a sparring session, I got partnered with a guy who had aggression issues. He's the guy at the academy who is super-cool in the changing room but as soon as sparring begins it's like you've just kidnapped his wife and children and unless he taps you out they won't be released. He goes nutso!

As per game plan he came at me like this was a life and death situation. We got into a scramble and I came out on his back and both hooks in position. Total accident with virtually no skill on my part, aside from an opportunity coming my way.

Wandering around the mat weaving in between the various fighters was another student from the academy, another white belt just ensuring that we didn't crack heads or steamroll the smaller guys. He was the overseer of safety.

I was working my game and looking to get a lapel choke, I had the guy on the right side when I noticed him glance up at the safety-guy wandering around who had stopped to watch us. The white belt who was standing looked down at my opponent nodded slightly as if agreeing to something. Unfortunately I had no clue what this meant, but it was a clear signal something was up. Before I had a chance to react the guy who's back I was controlling hooked his foot over my ankle and popped it. No warning. No tapping. Slam! Pop!

The sound was so loud that a guy near the entrance of the school ran over to check if it was broken, and we were in the middle of the mat. My foot didn't feel too bad, but went immediately white.

The professor teaching came over and told me to take a seat on the sidelines. I told him I was okay, it was just one of those things, but as soon as I stood to walk back to the bench I knew my ankle wasn't right. This didn't deter me and I kept a brave face. The guy who cracked it was very apologetic, I told him no need, its part of the game. He's a super nice guy just an all or nothing training partner.

But the event of it happening, with the subtle cue from the wandering white belt and the sudden smashing of my foot somehow irked me.

Next day, my foot had blown up to twice it's size and I spent the morning throwing up as my body went into shock, I should have predicted that.

No more training for me...for eight weeks.

This is not to impress you with my benevolence and immense sense of patience but to impress upon you that I could have taken another path and said 'Screw Jiu Jitsu it's not worth it'. My work suffered, I couldn't do things with my kids, my wife was pissed and wanted me to quit...but I didn't.

Understand this if you can:

This BJJ thing is important to your mental fortitude equally as much as your physical fortitude. You will get injuries and they will come from sometimes stupid scenarios. If this is an issue you can't accept then jiu jitsu may not be for you. Consider ping pong, that's much less stress on the joints.

Your attitude determines your altitude, according to those Success posters anyway and I believe that to be true.

TECHNIQUE CONCEPTS

ATTACK
"I am the greatest, I said that even before I knew I was."
~ Muhammad Ali - Boxing Legend

When in the white belt phase I think it is extremely important that you get a good grasp on the survival and escape tactics before you embark on the attack aspects. This doesn't mean you shouldn't attack but it means that you will be pushed into more survival aspects of the game by higher ranking fighters than you are going to steamroll lower belts. Let's face it, you are on the bottom rung trying to learn the basics, still, open sparring or specific training will be a reality.

I think it's important to cover some of the elements on attacks so that even while you are getting to grips with the fundamentals you can still get into the groove of some good habits and take them further into your training.

The following sections cover (not again, groan) Hip Control, Sweeps and Closed Guard Bottom. Of course having a guard game offers the ability to attack. One of the things I have tried to focus on with this volume is to keep things as straightforward and simple as possible so as not to confuse you.

I hope you don't think that this was going to be more in-depth as there are much better resources to delve deeper than this volume, as mentioned in the intro this is conceptual, not detail or technique driven. But, get a handle on the core concepts, and you can even start to develop your own details that work for you. This is what puts the 'art' in Martial Art and I don't feel there is a better way to express yourself than Brazilian jiu jitsu.

POSITION THEN SUBMISSION:
Don't try and submit your opponent from just anywhere. You must get yourself into a position of control first. This is referred to as Position, so things like side-control, mount, back-mount these are positions. Before position is usually Transition, this isn't the manual

to discuss transition. That will come later. But get used to Position then Submission.

Once in a tournament I tried to submit a guy with a cross collar choke that I had no business attempting as I was totally out of position. I had been drilling the cross collar choke with my professor and had it dialed in, yet for some reason I thought this meant that I could do it whenever I felt like. Listen up: You can't. You need to move into the correct position first, then the transition to the submission. There are no shortcuts here, so it's worth committing to memory. Position:Transition:Submission.

HIP CONTROL & GRIP CONTROL

I appreciate we have covered hip movement ad nauseam but we haven't much discussed grips and how they impact attack and defense. As we are in the attack section we can cover grips as they are applied to positions. The positions we will look at:

- Closed Guard

- Side Control

- Half Guard

- Mount

- Back

Of course there are many other positions you will be dealing with at a fundamental level but these will be the main ones, so don't start rushing off to master the reverse De La Riva just yet. Keep focused on these five. In this section we can take them apart one by one.

Before we do that, just note that they are all attack positions. So the closed guard is bottom. The mount is top and the back is back-control with hooks in. If you are not clear on these positions please talk to your coach, professor or refer to a reference manual like Saulo Ribiero's excellent primer Jiu Jitsu University.

Grip control is also covered in this area on attacking. Maybe there should have been an independent section on grips, they are that important, but for now let us not get bogged down in too much detail. We will cover grips in the various guard positions too.

CLOSED GUARD

On bottom and facing your opponent your hips need to be mobile. It's okay for your opponent to even lean forward placing all his weight through his hands onto your chest, but it's not okay if that weight transfers through the hips and locks you in place.

If weight transfers through your hip and pins you, the first action needs to be to break your opponents posture so he has to re-group. While he is re-grouping look to attack.

Has he dropped a hand to the mat? Go Kimura.

Has he raised his based away from his heels leaning forward? Scissor Sweep.

Has he pushed back keeping away from you with his balance moving away? Hip bump or sit-up sweep.

What about if his head comes forward and he tries to bury it in your stomach? Push one of his hands between your legs and go triangle or try a collar choke.

The options and outcomes are infinite, this is what makes it so interesting. Now, just go back and review those techniques (provided you know what they are), every one of the attacks needs the hips to be available to move and oftentimes move quickly.

It is impossible to attack from your back without free hips. Always keep that in mind when you are using the closed guard.

Also keep your grips in position. Try to make it a habit that neither of your hands should be empty at any time. It's just a good habit to get into and when breaking your opponents posture, breaking grips is also a key element in that.

Marcelo Garcia never lets anyone get grips on him, even if he is in mid transition and his technique is coming together, he will stop, break grips and then continue. This demonstrates how important the grip is in achieving victory.

For you as a white belt, victory is in controlling the action. Again, this is a good habit to get into, if you control the action you will have a good chance of controlling the outcome. If you feel your opponent is imposing his game on you and you have the attacking posture then you need to move the action back to you controlling. How do you do this? Break his posture and start moving your hips. Again, simple, but not easy.

HALF GUARD

Half guard bottom has a very similar prescription to the closed guard with the exception that it is a far more aggressive attacking guard. There are many more sweeps and half guard variations as you get more advanced.

If you want to take your half guard to a whole new level then there are two DVD sets that come to mind: 111 Half Guard Techniques with Caio Terra and Jeff Glovers' Deep Half Guard. Both available on Amazon.

Grips with a half guard are not as important as the closed guard. For me, the main focus of my hands when I am in half guard is to ensure my opponent doesn't get head control and I keep an underhook. If he gets head control and flattens me out then I have to recover full guard or go for a sweep...which is duplicating work and effort so I would rather not, and I would rather you not too.

Once you move into an attacking position, taking the underhook initiative for example, then having grips becomes essential. Again, try to fill your hands once you decide to attack.

If you are not quite sure what the 'underhook initiative' is then ask a coach or your professor how you get the underhook when in half guard and I am sure they will be happy to demonstrate.

MOUNT

This is one of the most difficult attacking positions that a white belt can handle. The Upa (or hip bump) seems to be a technique that is very effective. Most white belts managing the feat of getting into top mount don't seem to stay on top long before they get bumped.

Why is this?

Usually their base and their hips are in the wrong position. Have you ever noticed that when a black belt gets in the mount they are eager to climb higher and get their knees under their opponent's armpits. This is the correct position for the hip, as the opponent's hips can raise now and there is no contact with the black belts hip. Whereas, if you mount and in effect you are hip to hip he can bump you.

Most white belts look to attack right away, this makes them rise up in the air so their head is high vertically and their hips are low. The base is compromised here, and that's what makes the Upa so effective.

Landing in mount, first, stabilize your position. Get head control and then lock your feet under (behind) your opponents knees (as if getting closed guard from the top mount), keep your hands out wide, spread wide open. This should bring the position under control while your opponent thrashes around underneath you. The hips are still connected but the arms and locked feet will clamp with great effectiveness. You should look like 'Y' shape on top.

Once they are growing weary of bumping and looking for options, bring a hand in quickly and wrap it around your opponents' neck gaining head control. Simultaneously shift your weight (chest) to the side with the outstretched arm.

This usually gets the reaction that the Upa is now available, he will clamp the arm that just wrapped and try to bump to that side, but due to the mechanics of you moving your weight (chest) to the opposite side, a cantilever is formed and you cannot be bumped in that direction. He can't bump you the other way, your arm is still extended as a post. So he drops back again trying to come up with plan C.

This is now is the ideal time to hoist a knee under the armpit of his arm that is planted against your head-control arm. Stay low and plant your foot into his ribs pushing your groin almost onto his neck. That's how high up you want to be.

Do the same on the other side and keep your head low, not upright, you should be sliding over him. You should now be in a safe position regardless of how much he tries to push you off. If he extends an arm, it's yours. Personally in such a dominant position I try a couple of arm attacks to distract him enough to go straight for the neck.

The hips need to be high on your opponent though, so they are not connected.

There is an alternative to this. There is an alternative to everything in jiu jitsu and that is to keep the hips connected and ride out the upa with a free flowing movement. I have seen this work very effectively but it never worked as well as getting the hips into a heavier more controlling position.

You may have noticed that grips do not really form a part of the position here as the hands are used mostly to base. This is correct, the grips only work once you are on the attack and even then they are more like hooks than grips for the most part.

The hip is far more important in the mount position, and using the feet as grips is an even better example. If you can lock your feet or grapevine as soon as you mount then this will allow some precious seconds for that stabilization process to take place. The grips in the mount are your hips and your feet. Use them in that order.

IMAGE COURTESY OF QWERTYJUTSU.COM

BACK CONTROL

When you have back control, hooks in, then your hip should naturally be on the same alignment as your opponents. This is where you start and keeping that level is important to you keeping in control.

You can try this: If you are specific training on back control and your partner starts on your back with hooks in, then as soon as you go, just scoot down so your hips move away from him. This is a great back defense starting position. Conversely you can push back against him so he is on his back with your weight is on top of him, this again makes it difficult for him to get any kind of collar grips, position or choose the side he will need to drop you to in order to get the choke.

Notice all it takes is to move the hips in a direction that doesn't suit him and he will run out of ideas real quick.

If you have back control keep the hips in line, this should provide a nice alignment for a choke too. If he scoots down as mentioned above then you will need to move more toward an arm attack as the angle for the choke will be compromised.

The seat belt grip is a perfect starting position for back control with hooks. This is the position where you have one arm over the shoulder and one arm beneath the armpit of the opposite arm with the hands clasped together pulling your opponent in tight - elbows back and down. Your chest and his back should be glued together, this will enable masterful control and make it very difficult to escape.

Also with the seat belt, collar grips and wrist control are right there. You don't need to be peeking over your opponents shoulder to see what's happening at the front, with the seatbelt everything becomes much more tactile. As he moves you can sense it and counter, if he tries to scoot and the seatbelt is tight, no way, he'll choke himself or present an arm attack. Learn the seatbelt and keep the hips aligned, they go hand in hand.

SWEEPS

Sweeping your opponent is essential to gaining top attacking positions. Let's take a quick look at the dominant top positions:
- Side Control

- Mount

- Back

- Knee on Belly

When you pass someone's guard and land in side control, in competition you will be awarded three points. Four points for the mount or the back, and sometimes one leads to the other. You could also pick up a quick two points for knee-on-belly facing your opponent, oddly enough you get no points for knee-on-belly facing away from your opponent (as of this writing).

Why is it that if we land in our opponents closed guard, half guard or get to his back with no hooks that we don't get points or advantages? They are not dominant positions because you can't control the attack from there, all you can do is break guard or try and get hooks. These are considered to be 'neutral positions'.

This boils down to the fact then that we need a method, regardless of our position, to get to one of those dominant positions as effectively as possible: Enter the sweep.

Let's just say your opponent breaks your guard and starts to pass. One of the first techniques you will learn is to get to half-guard at all costs, in an attempt to stop or at least delay the pass. This is good advice. Especially as the half guard bottom, in my opinion, is as effective as the closed guard and is a very offensive position. The half guard as an attack position is littered with sweep opportunities. Once the sweep begins then you should control your opponent in a way so as to land in one of the dominant positions. Two points for the sweep and you now have attacking options.

The hips and grips, yet again, play a part in all sweeps. In fact I would say that if you have a deft hip then a bottom guard, sweep game might be a winner for you. A teammate of mine has been getting away with the bottom guard, sweep to a dominant position and then racking up points for years, and been successful with it.

Doesn't submit many opponents but can train long and hard gaining dominant position one after the other. It works.

CLOSED GUARD BOTTOM (AGAIN)

Closed Guard bottom is going to be your bread and butter attacking position at white belt that's why I covered it twice here. Almost all positions stem from your CG Bottom. Think about it. Mount if you wrapped your legs around your opponent or locked ankles is very similar in nature, so is Back Mount hooks in. It's an incredibly dominant attacking position.

Your hips engaged at the same level and this gives you the element of control, so try to get your closed guard game together as this is possibly the most important 'stance' in Jiu Jitsu. It also comes into play much more in No-Gi jiu jitsu, which you may enjoy as you advance.

Being able to flow from one technique to another is the mark of a quality jiu jitsu player. This comes with time as each position begins to feel comfortable. In the previous manual Zen Jiu Jitsu I discussed how there are many parallels to Human chess with BJJ, this is especially true when it comes to linking techniques together. If you are on bottom in the closed guard you have the major advantage of knowing that your opponent only has one objective: break your guard. Some people will call out passing as being the objective, but one cannot happen without the other one first.

Your opponent, on the other hand, has no idea what you plan to do to attack. There is obviously the stumbling block in the bottom game of there being so many ways to break guard, but this is at least finite. And although the techniques from the bottom are also finite they are far more expansive, with counters to counters to various guard games evolving into different guards. Trust me, get a good solid closed guard bottom and you will always have a solid attacking position to fall back on (pun intended).

DEFENSE

In this section on defense I want you to consider what defense is. It is moving from an inferior position to an improved position or a position of transition to a dominant position - hope that makes sense. We discussed the dominant positions in the section on Sweeps, in this section it means you need to defend against each of those positions. Quick recap:

- Side Control

- Mount

- Back

- Knee on Belly

If you remain under the pressure of one of these positions for too long you will only create more opportunities for your opponent that will ultimately lead to your submission. Your ability to defend in jiu jitsu is essential at white belt, as the time will come when you move up to blue and start sparring with purple and brown belts the number of submission attempts can be relentless so learning to have a solid defense is a priority at this stage in your development.

The first step in Defense is Survival (we will cover that next).

SURVIVAL

"Adopt the Survival mindset. Stop trying to beat anyone and everyone. Just don't lose anymore."
~ Helio Gracie - Co-Creator of Gracie Jiu Jitsu

When you are studying at the white belt level the most important factor is the act of survival. This is pretty much a given, on your first day you probably aren't sure what's going on and the only option is sink or swim, I would be very surprised if you started beating people on your first day on the mat.

Even though you got involved with jiu jitsu to learn submissions. The key issue as a white belt is to survive first, and then you can move into more favorable positions. This is also a good test of your attitude towards training and training partners. The process of being patient and letting your ego get a good stomping are real tests at this stage. I have seen many students who were very successful off the mat get into trouble on their first training session and crumble. As time wears on and they realize that they don't know very much their insecurities of being on the mat subside and they accept that surviving a training session is of the utmost importance.

Learning to survive is probably the most valuable lesson jiu jitsu has to offer.

As time goes on don't forget that you will be learning more than just survival tactics, you will learn attacks as well as defenses, just remember as a white belt the defense element is more valuable right now. It teaches patience and the ability to leave your ego at the studio door. Very valuable lessons I'm sure you agree.

Learn to tap as mentioned earlier, and learn to tap often. It's okay to tap, it just means your partner won that point, now we can reset and go again. It is the ultimate learning tool.

Some people think that this concept is ridiculous and that survival cannot be the foundation of jiu jitsu. All you need to do is analyze the origins of jiu jitsu and it's obvious that survival techniques were the cornerstone of the all the original Gracie wins. As a student ages he no longer has the will to compete at a younger level as time takes a toll. This is when their earlier survival foundation comes into play. The use of space and negative space are even more apparent and the older students can frustrate the younger more athletic fighters using these two principles. Using defense strategies age becomes less of a factor in any match.

BREAKING THE GUARD AND PASSING

One of the key principles that a lot of white belts misunderstand in the concept of guard breaking and passing is that it isn't a fair fight. It's you and gravity against the guy in the guard. When passing always bear this in mind, and don't bother to use muscle, your old friend gravity will do the work. This is the theory and if I am able to drive my weight forward toward your body then I should be able to pass your guard. That's a fact.

PROGRESSION

This again is a progression from the original concepts mentioned earlier: position, transition, submission. You still need all these elements to get gravity on your side and make the maximum impact with the minimum effort. If you set up the pass properly and are in the right position with the right angle (hips and grips in place) then you can start to move into a more dominant position (transition) this is usually where most white belts either get caught out and the opponent escapes or they don't pass, give up and return to the guard - reset.

If you track back I'll bet it was down to the original position (angle, hips, grips) being wrong that prevented you from passing. The first step in the set up for the pass is to stop your opponent being where he wants to be at any time. Make him uncomfortable. If he imposes his guard on you then you need to play his game, you need to measure and anticipate his next moves. You won't need your defense techniques if you don't allow your opponent to get into an attacking position. You won't need to solve that issue if it doesn't even crop up, and that's where your initial position will come in.

If something is happening to you on the mat that you don't like and your opponent is getting his grips and hips in place. Get out of there and reset. There is no rule in jiu jitsu that you have to allow your opponent or training partner to work his game on you. It's the opposite – you should be working your game. If you allow your partner to take his moves too far and he pushes you into a position that you are swept or you need to tap, then tap or accept the sweep. He deserves the 'W'.

Learn to move into a position of control first. Make it difficult for your opponent to put you into his game – don't forget, it's all grips and hips at this point.

PACE

As with all the other elements mentioned above you need to control the pace and rate at which you pass. A lot of white belts tend to rush the pass at the transition phase and this leads to holes being created (space) and then an escape. You must be the one dictating the pace and then putting on the controls. Side control isn't called side mount, it's named <u>control</u> for a reason. When you pass, stabilize. If you fail to do this then you fall back into your opponents' game.

OTHER GUARDS

As your game develops you will begin to see other guards in play, even if you are a four stripe white belt, your handle on an open guard game will invariably be limited.

It may not, but as we discussed earlier having a killer closed guard game should be your first port of call. Don't run into the dreaded guard-accumulation game, this is a dead-end, I promise you.

At the academy you'll see some guys, I call them 'technique accumulators', they are the guys with all the books, DVD's and enough YouTube subscriptions to give a regular person a migraine. If you have some open-mat time they are usually trying some technique way above their pay-grade. This is not the way to naturally develop into a good BJJ player. Focusing on the fundamentals at white belt is key, though the tractor beam of fancy-shmancy moves is very potent.

And with that in mind, I still want to briefly touch on the other guards. What they are, how they work and how they can improve your game...in the future. For now as you move towards blue belt focus on the closed guard and maybe some basic half guard escapes to full guard. That's a solid plan.

HALF GUARD (ZEE GUARD)

This is very much a go to move for most players as it has a lot of possibilities and the opportunity to get into it in a sparring session is good. At the white belt level the most common method of getting into the half guard is when your opponent tries to pass your guard and you use your legs to defend snatching one of his legs into your half. You use your thighs to grab onto one of his legs, so one of your thighs will be in between his legs and one of your thighs will be against his outer thigh or over his hip creating space between you.

Note: It doesn't matter if you cross your ankles, leave them open or figure four your legs, if one of your thighs is in the middle of your opponents thighs: you are in half guard.

I feel this is a good guard to focus on all the way through to brown belt as there are a lot of options for attacks, defenses and counters. Plus it is an easy guard to get into if this is the game you plan to work.

For now, I would like you to focus on two things. If you are in half guard and your opponent flattens you on to your back then you MUST have a strategy to recover to full guard and/or back to a spacious half guard (Zee Guard). This depends too on whether they have you flattened with head control or not. But you need to have that recovery mechanism in place before you get to blue belt.

Also, it is important that you have a killer half guard pass. Think about the comments above, you will often find yourself in half guard top or half guard bottom. Half guard bottom you have lots of possibilities (sweeps, back-takes, submissions, etc.) but Half guard top is not in one of the dominant position classifications (although you can submit from here) so you need to improve your position to mount, back, side-control or knee-on-belly, and you can only do this if you release the leg that's trapped. So, you need a good half guard escape in your toolkit.

I like the half guard escapes demonstrated by Caio Terra in the excellent DVD set Modern Jiu Jitsu. It's worth the cost and is available from Amazon.

OPEN GUARD

If you don't have your ankles locked around your opponents waist but are still facing him then you have an open guard. At white belt it's more a case of stopping your opponent passing by moving to half guard or back to full guard. You don't want to start building an open guard game unless it is a transition to a closed guard position.

This may sound like it's holding you back but let's not encourage confusion before you start working on your super-duper tornado guard. I just want to use this section to clarify the open guard as you move to Blue, then you can start working on some open guard strategies.

Let's look at a couple of open guard options merely as an introduction then if a higher ranking student pulls one of these on you at least you will know what it is.

SPIDER GUARD

Probably the most common open guard used in BJJ. This is best described as gripping both sleeves (or a sleeve and collar) while pressing both feet on the hips or the biceps, causing your opponents posture to break and balance to shift into a precarious position. It's a natural position to move into from the closed guard and very popular due to its range of sweeps and attack positions.

When your guard starts to become more open and flexible the spider-guard will more than likely be your first go-to open guard. You can then get more creative from there. Ask your coaches and professors to maybe show you an attack or two from the spider guard as this can sometimes be a position you might fall into if your guard breaks.

IMAGE COURTESY OF GRAPPLEARTS.COM

DLR (DE LA RIVA)

This is a far more advanced guard system. And it truly is a system. There are a great number of options and derivatives here, from the Reverse De La Riva to the Berimbolo, which have been spawned by this guard. Originally invented by Ricardo De La Riva to help him train against an academy full of much larger training partners it is now a staple in the advanced BJJ curriculum.

The position is to lasso your leg around your opponents' leg so that your foot hooks from the outside into their groin or inner thigh. The opposite foot can rest on their inner thigh, hip or even on the floor, the controlling element is the foot active in the lasso's as this creates many of the attacking options or sweeps. The hands are gripping a sleeve or collar and a hand will be gripping the ankle of the leg inside the lasso. See the image below:

Image courtesy of Wikipedia.com

You will note that this is an incredibly complex guard and an extremely difficult one to pass if the guard player is accomplished in using it. The thing that makes it so difficult are the number of blocking elements: each grip is on a collar, sleeve or ankle, each foot is wrapped tightly around a leg or pressing the balance to move the opponent into danger. To make an effective pass against this guard each one of these roadblocks needs to be disabled or deflected and neutralized in some way and this can be very hard work when your posture is bent so badly.

Let's not get too deep in to the DLR from here, there will be plenty of time to look at that when you are working through to purple belt.

SIDE CONTROL

This, like the mount, is a difficult position for a white belt to decipher and maintain. The retention of this position becomes more a feat of strength than a feat of technique and this is where most white belts go wrong.

Again, we need to prepare and consider the bio-mechanical action of the side control.

- It is one of the most dominant positions, so you should be able to attack from here.

- Your opponent should not easily be able to replace his guard.

- You should be able to control this position as you transition to something more favorable, e.g. the back or the mount.

So, how do we achieve the items above? Let's look at physiology:

1. You have your weight on top and are pressing into your opponent.

2. The hips of your opponent are controlled. Achieved by 'caging' the hips or using a hand or knee to block. Recovery back to full guard is prevented.

3. In an ideal situation you have head and arm control. This is usually a secondary consideration to controlling the hips.

When moving to side control make sure you are pressing horizontally and get one of your knees beneath their knees, so that their kneecaps face away from you. This puts a lot of pressure on your opponents' hips and spine making it very difficult to recover back to half or full closed guard.

If (once you have the hips isolated) you press on to the head and arm control. This is the makings of good side control. Control is the operative word here. This is not a position that you can afford to have loose in any way as your opponent knows this is a dominant position and nothing good can come from staying in this position, so they will buck and hip escape until their energy levels become too low.

Most white belts don't take enough time to stabilize this (or any) position. Remember we talked about this in Core Principles (a lot) - Position, Transition, Submission. Well, the position element is important to gain that level of control BEFORE you move to the transition. What happens often with new players is that they are happy with the fact they have passed successfully that they move to the transition too soon and then their opponent escapes easily. Stabilize the position first before moving.

HIP CONTROL ON TOP

There are two main methods of controlling the hip in side control top, one is using the knee and the other is using the hand as a blocking mechanism.

Using the knee to block the hips is essential as sometimes you will need both hands at head level to attack or provide head control, especially if the opponent is stronger. The hand to block the hip is also a pre-requisite in side control as this prevents guard recovery and also allows you to spin north/south or switch your base with out landing yourself in full or half guard.

Concentrate on keeping your opponent <u>controlled</u> when you pass to side.

As a side note there is another type of hip control that is usually referred to as 'caging the hips'. This is a very effective method of controlling the hips and can be used to stall the action if you feel you are tiring or gassing out. This is a combination of the knee and arm.

This time your knee would slide underneath the back of the knee of your opponent and your upper body would clamp down over his hips with your arm pushing into the opposite side of his hip. This basically causes the hips to be neutralized between your elbow and your knee as you trap his knees between, effectively caging the hips with your mid-section. This can work extremely well and even now as a more experienced fighter I usually cage the hips first before moving to the more attacking form of side control.

HEAD CONTROL

Head Control. One of the first things I like to see white belts do is get comfortable with head control. This is more a question of making your opponent look away from you using your shoulder. This is not a strength thing. I see it a lot with white belts coming from a wrestling background, they tend to just get a headlock and hang on as if their lives depended on it. This makes it easier to escape believe it or not. Okay, it might put a little more cauliflower on the ear of their training partner but they will more than likely get out.

Now if you use the shoulder to push the jaw away from the person on bottom this causes a spinal twist that transfers down the body and thereby begins the isolation of the hips (there's the hip again, you didn't think I would leave it out?!). This doesn't use as much strength but feels like a ton of pressure if applied correctly.

This makes for effective head control and is an important part of maintaining side control.

TACTICAL CONSIDERATIONS

"Do not fear the man who has thrown 10,000 kicks. Fear the man who has thrown one kick 10,000 times."
~ Bruce Lee - Creator of Jeet Kune Do

PROMOTIONS

Promotions are merely milestones, don't become too attached to them. Quick anecdote. I was invited to a large promotional ceremony when I was a much junior belt and it was going to be a big event. End of year awards were to be given out, citations and promotions with some senior belts being promoted even higher.

I was long overdue a stripe but was told by one of the coaches that it would be best to delay it for the big event. Sounded pretty cool. The promotion I had been told was late due to the professors at the school being away on business. Again, I was cool with that as it meant by the time the ceremony came around I was due to get two stripes, which would have made it quite an occasion for me.

The day rolled around and the academy was packed. There was a mini-seminar and then some sparring before we broke up and got settled for the promotions.

One of my training buddies had started around the same time as me, but couldn't dedicate as much time so I had surpassed him a little in terms of technique but he was still really good, we were both doing well. The difference was he turned up for class just before the professor left for his business trip so he got the stripe I was missing. He's a super cool guy, good friend and great training partner, we both knew that we were the same rank in theory. And with the ceremony the balance would be put right.

I'm sure you can guess what happened. The event went well but when I stepped up for my promotion, only one stripe managed it's way onto my belt, with my training buddy getting another, so he was now a stripe ahead and I felt left way behind.

To add insult to injury, some of my teammates who had begun training much later than me also got promoted as a surprise. So not only were my peers moving further ahead, the guys I was past in terms of time had almost caught up to me in rank!

I was pissed off.

Why though? Had my game changed? Was I suddenly worse than when I walked on to the mat that day? Had my training partners suddenly become much better than me?

Obviously none of that was true, so why did I feel so hard done by? We, as westerners, become too attached to our status and the perception of belt color is no exception to our ego driven society.

In reality we need to get some perspective and not even look at the color of our belts...or other students.

If you are a white belt, don't feel intimidated when you roll with a blue belt, just imagine he's a white belt like you - he was once.

With my own professor when we roll, sometimes we both try really hard and it's tough (he kills me often and I've never come even close to improving on him) but even when I sweep him or move into a dominant position he smiles and tells me that it's good. He doesn't pull on his game-face and turn it into the world championships, its not about level or colors to him, it's about improvement.

Since my promotional epiphany I don't even think about promotions any more. If they come then I am grateful, if they don't ... I am still grateful for BJJ being in my life. I can't lose.

There is another element to consider about promotions that you won't even think about yet. When you get promoted to a higher rank there is a weird sense of responsibility. When you move up to blue its like you can longer accept being subbed by a white belt, or even having your guard passed. If it does happen then that feels like some kind of personal defeat.

We strut our stuff. And then eventually get promoted to purple and the same happens, those pesky blue belts better not even TRY to pass our guard. It's okay if a brown or black belt passes though. This is complete B.S. and we should stop it.

This ego trip stopped around purple, or it did with me. The responsibility I feel now is only with myself to improve and at the very least try and stop plateaus...though that's almost impossible. You need to be able to pace your progress and forget the belt rankings.

Honestly, they are not that important.

INJURIES

Unfortunately, one of the biggest reasons that students wash out of Brazilian Jiu Jitsu is due to injuries. Injury management will be part of your long-term game plan and needs to be managed.

The most common injuries:

- Shoulders

- Knees

- Ribs

- Fingers

It seems joints get the roughest ride from BJJ, or cartilage related body parts.

In all cases try to keep the ice on them for a period of twenty-four hours after the injury. Don't go for too much heat at this point until the inflammation is under control. This would be in a cycle of ice for five minutes, then remove the ice and allow recovery for fifteen minutes followed by ice for five. Keep this going. Before bed have something to eat and then load up the ibuprofen (do not exceed the prescribed dose on the container - need I add I am not a doctor).

This should reduce inflammation, which is a good and bad thing. You need the inflammation to heal but you need to reduce it to manage the pain.

The odd thing is that the injuries mentioned above are pretty much all self inflicted or not normally damaged by an external force. Most submissions come by neck or arm, so you would expect that neck, bicep and elbow injuries be predominant due to the stress applied, but it doesn't seem to be the case. We push out of mount too hard and a shoulder pops. We try to scissor sweep a guy two hundred pounds heavier than us and a knee pops. My last rib injury happened when I was trying a De La Riva sweep and pushed my body into a weird angle - pop! Super painful.

Of course there are times when opponents (usually accidentally) do cause a little damage. One of the times an ankle popped was due to a footballer tackling me while kneeling, I fell backwards and my feet stayed put. Not cool. But I recovered, and you will too.

All my injuries sustained over the years have recovered to full or better condition than before, and I have never had surgery for any injuries (touch wood). I would encourage you to resist surgery as much as possible, I appreciate that this is sometimes unavoidable, but one thing I have noticed over the years with all the various training partners I have had. Once the surgeries begin they never train the same way again, even after full recovery. It's as if they are always aware that another surgery could happen and they don't press as hard or train as hard as they did.

Rest and Recuperation is always an alternative. I appreciate that this can be difficult, if not excruciating, to see your training partners rolling and having a great time while you feel sidelined and they are improving. But this jiu jitsu thing is a long-term proposition. It's not a shot at the title and then go do something else. This is something that I hope to be doing into my seventies and eighties, and I hope you will too.

Of all the injuries I have sustained my back has been the worst. This was a herniated disc and not actually down to BJJ but down to deadlifting in an attempt to improve my top game. I (mistakenly) thought deadlifting would build my back and make it stronger.

Although this wasn't caused by jiu jitsu, the point I am making is that to this day I have adapted my game to ensure that my back is protected. My double leg looks a little odd and is certainly not text book, but it's effective and I feel no pressure on my lower back. You may need to adapt too if an injury is long term or is painful to complete the technique the traditional way.

If you have an injury that is long term and could knock you out of training if a flare up occurs then you need to adapt the technique. Talk to your coaches and professor about any injuries that you may have and what you can do about it.

When I did my ribs, the best advice I could get was to rub barbecue sauce on them. Apparently its good on ribs - kidding - don't rub barbecue sauce on your body unless you're into that kind of thing. The point being made was, there are some body parts that when injured don't have adaptations. They are an essential part of the BJJ game, unavoidable. You need to rest - no discussion necessary.

And don't forget, you can quickly escape from any technique applied to you...just two small taps and you're out.

COMPETITION

"Those skilled in combat do not become angered, those who are skilled at winning do not become afraid."
Morihei Ueshiba - Father of Aikido

Remember, you don't have to compete, it's not essential but it can be a good test of many skills not just your jiu jitsu. As I mentioned in Zen Jiu Jitsu Volume One, I'm not a 'feelin' it' kind of competitor.

In fact nerves really take a toll on me and I feel pretty awful from the minute I sign up until the final match is over. I've taken steps to quell this as best I can, and even though I am prepared much better these days I still feel nerves until I engage with my opponent.

When I was younger I boxed quite a bit and was also very active in the Karate scene with competitions. It was the same then, nerves overtook. Then one year I decided to really pick one tournament and train hard for it, really focus on this one tournament. It was a national junior championship, so I dedicated myself to technique and fitness. Over the next three month my game and confidence grew, I felt amazing, then the day of the competition came.

We drove the one hundred and fifty miles to the venue and set up camp, several members of my team were also competing, which is great to work in a team atmosphere but, to me at least, increases the pressure. When my time finally came to step on the mat, my opponent looked ready and although I felt the nerves there was a strange side effect from all the hard work. I was also equally confident. This seemed to be the realization that I could not have prepared or trained any harder, everything led to this moment.

Did I win? No. I was disqualified in the quarterfinals for excessive contact. This was tournament Karate and not boxing, but when I got back my team were really impressed with my event performance. Everyone clapped and cheered as I reached the stand, even some of our competitive teams came over and shook my hand. I felt vindicated for my previous nervous endeavors.

The moral of the story is this, if you are fully prepared and you have practiced, and drilled technique to the best of your ability then it doesn't matter whether you win or lose. You have already won. It is impossible not to be a better BJJ practitioner after the match...win or lose.

One year I snagged a really odd injury to my groin about a week before the Pan Ams. It wasn't serious but the pain was one of the worst I had felt when my leg rotated in the socket so any kind of guard game - even closed guard - was out. I had to concede that this was not going to be my year, and dropped out forgoing my entry fee.

When my groin healed (it takes several months to even walk normally) I was in much better condition technique-wise. All the training leading up to the Pans was not forgotten, it was all still in my brain. My timing was a little rusty but within two or three weeks I was pretty much back and giving everyone a run for their money again.

YOUR FIRST TOURNAMENT

"In fighting and in everyday life you should be determined though calm."

Miyamoto Musashi - Swordsman and Samurai Master

Be wise. Don't rush in.

Are you ready for another short story of woe? Here is a rundown of my first tournament experience.

I was a white belt (like you are) and was training fairly steadily. Still new to the school but really enjoying it, full of positive energy and keen to learn. Over a period of weeks I met another guy who grew up not far from my hometown, so we trained a little together and then decided to take some privates and split the bill. The privates were pretty pricey back then, I was on a budget, so this partnership worked for me.

The private classes went really well and my game was clicking into place for my level. We sparred at the end of every private and much to the professors and coaches amusement we always started sparring standing up. Being about the same weight helped, and we both grew up in tough part of town so it was no problem.

My training partner was real aggressive (still is) but my technique was getting better and I kept coming out on top with a sub or a points win. Either way I got the 'W' and he got a good workout.

On the school notice board a sign went up declaring that there would be a BJJ tournament at a college close by. It was a short drive to a small college so I thought maybe this would be a good testing ground for my new techniques. Get my feet wet, so to speak.

My training partner told me he fancied this tournament, I told him the same that I was 'up for it.' So we both registered and paid our entry fees. We carried on training and were excited about the upcoming tournament that was about six weeks away. I had been training about two months at this point in time, and was pretty impressed with my progress. Hubris!

We also kept the privates and sparring sessions going, which was great training for the tournament. Then tournament day swung around.

Let me qualify this. About two days before the tournament I decided to cut some weight, it wasn't too successful either. I don't have any wrestling background or experience of weight cutting, so the day before the tournament I felt a little weak and sick. But I was good to go, no way I was backing out. My training partner called and told me he was ready to rock, I agreed (though a little queasy) that I felt the same.

Nerves started kicking in the night before the big day causing me to sleep poorly. The next morning was worse. My bracket was scheduled for three in the afternoon, so I had all the morning and lunchtime to brood over the impending battle and my confidence began to slide.

I drove to the college where the competition was being held, a banner emblazoned above the doorway read 'Grapplers Quest' that should have been some kind of omen. Regardless I checked in and grabbed my free Competitor tee-shirt. Inside I tried to find my training buddy but there was no sign of him, not only that, there was no sign of anyone else from my academy. I wasn't sure why, but it seemed unpopular with the more experienced students. I found out why a little later.

Then the really bad news came in, I got a text from my training partner that he wouldn't be able to make it, something had cropped up. Totally on my own at this point, unsure on how a BJJ competition worked, I got changed and started warming up.

I was called to the administration table and told that my bracket was empty, there was no one in my age range available to compete. In fact, there was no one in the bracket below that one either so I dropped down two age groups to get a match or else it was a waste of time. I told them I was a Go. They dropped me the two brackets and I was the oldest man in my bracket now by around twenty years.

We were pulled into the corral, our names called so we had to step onto the scales. I was just under the mark. Then led like men to the gallows to mat number five. I was making a little conversation with the kid beside me who just kept scowling and grunting. Totally unaware that we would be fighting in three minutes time.

We both had our names called, I shook hands, he pretty much pulled away and took his grappler stance (at this point in time I didn't even know what a grappler stance was). Referee called for us to fight and this guy rushed me, I danced back and he pulled guard.

Locked in his closed guard, I was confident I could pass. Broke his guard, he flipped into a triangle I escaped, he pursued it and swept me then mounted me. He eventually got the tap with a triangle from mount.

Walking off the mat I felt like I had been fucked by a hurricane. Bewildered and shocked by the whole ordeal I just wanted to go home and lick my wounds. Not so fast. This was a double elimination gig, I had to fight one more time.

I kept massaging my forearms, which now felt like they should belong to Popeye then sat at the side of the mat waiting for the next executioners call, I tried (quite desperately) to pull my shit together. Watching the other matches intently I attempted to compose myself. A game plan formed in my mind, I would jump guard this time. That was it. Nothing else came. But I knew in my next match I would jump guard.

Sure enough, my name was called, and then my opponent stepped out. Young Japanese guy, very respectful, we shook and the ref called 'fight'. We circled for a second, then I jumped guard. I really looked like I knew what I was doing at this point, my legs clamped tight, I fell in for a sweep but he dropped to his knees. Slipping my right hand in deep I tried the cross-collar choke, and although I thought I had him, it was too loose. He broke my guard and started to pass (my bottom game was really crap), he made it to half guard my grips broke and he attacked. I sort of escaped then he took my back submitting me with a bow and arrow choke.

I didn't mind tapping.

Glad it was over, the sensation of relief was amazing, truly amazing. The sense of comradeship when the tournament was over was also an enlightening experience. I had been summarily beaten - twice, and yet walked out of the hall feeling like a superstar. It was tough, it was rough, but it was fantastic.

On speaking to other competitors over the years I have asked about nerves and controlling the body. Even in an interview Caio Terra he told me that the nerves never go away, they are better on some days than others but they never evaporate completely. I find this very interesting.

What other elements did I glean from this experience:

1. Not all ranks are the same. On talking to the other competitors who by now, mainly due to my age and lack of experience, felt sorry for me and chatted quite openly. Every white belt I spoke to had been training at least a year and one had been training almost two years. Just because they wear a white belt doesn't mean that their professor uses the same promotional system as your own school.

Personally, I feel this is a little like sandbagging, but it's not regulated so be on the lookout for people who look a little too good. When I was a purple belt I fought a guy who had been purple for ten years. I got the upper hand in that battle but still, it was an interesting few minutes of combat. The guy was just too good, he made a simple error due to over-confidence maybe, and that cost him. That was all I needed. I was terrified, the guys stand up game was judo black belt level.

2. All tournaments are not created equal. The reason that the more advanced guys at the gym avoided this competition was that the Grapplers Quest circuit is pretty high level. It's more advanced and runs a bunch of excellent Gi and No-Gi tournaments. They are always well turned out with real competitors, who are looking to test their skills, even at white belt. This is the kind of competition that is not for the faint hearted.

The biggest problem with any tournament outside of the IBJJF is that the rankings are not in anyway standardized. You are thinking that you are going to compete against someone of a similar age, rank and weight. The age and weight are fairly binary considerations. But rank, that becomes a little more subjective. Some academies have seven year blue belts, some academies have five year black belts. I'm not sure what the actual process is supposed to be or if the Gracie family wanted to use a standard. As far as I am aware the only federation putting any kind of information on belt promotions out there is the IBJJF. My academy uses these guidelines, so technically if they are followed to the letter and based on time and attendance you could achieve a black belt in eight years. This seems appropriate to me. It could take some students longer but the time period could be no shorter.

The fact remains that you should have the basics mastered by continual attendance and improvement on the mat for a minimum of eight years. In effect you should be at a black belt level in BJJ. Okay, not world champ level but black belt, yes, the math works.

So if someone has been a blue belt for say five years and a purple for two then (according to the IBJJF promotion regulation) you have a black belt competitor fighting in a purple belt division. Just my take on the current competition situation. Food for thought.

FAILURE IS AN OPTION

I know this is counter to confidence building but I heard Chael Sonnen say this on a recent Ultimate Fighter show. He was making the statement that the term 'Failure is not an option' was plenty gung-ho but not realistic. You need to be aware that you are entering into a fight, you need to be prepared that the guy (or girl) you are up against is also trying to win equally, with the same amount of intensity and fury that you are bringing to the table. This is not table tennis!

This is **REAL**.

You don't need the platitudes of self-talk because when you are in the fray they will not and cannot come to your aid. This is what you need to concentrate on as you fill in the registration form for your tournament: Have I prepared for this as well as I could have done?

If the answer to that question is Yes, then go ahead and sign up. If there is a nagging voice at the back of your mind telling you that you had flu for two weeks, then that ankle injury kept you off the mat plus that heavy duty project at work was a real slog so no wonder you missed a few competition classes. Then pass. No shame in that. There will be another tournament, next week, next month, even next year.

Visualizing yourself on the podium will not take you past the lack of training no matter how many times you play that winning show reel. If you have the time on the mat, and you have been training consistently, feel good, feel confident then go for it. It's scary when you feel prepared and that fear never really falls away (I discuss this more in Zen Jiu Jitsu) but it can be a whole lot worse when you don't feel the fear and have some confidence that you can win but haven't put the time in on the mat. This can get real scary, real quick as the realization of your lack of preparation sets in.

There is no rush, take your time. You can do this and do it well.

TRAINING AIDS

Unlike a lot of other manuals on jiu jitsu I do think that training aids can really help. There are only a couple that work really well in my opinion and they don't need to be purchased at the white belt level with the exception of the training journal. Whether you use a fully fledged training system journal or just a regular notebook from the supermarket, this is an essential part of your development as a fighter.

The three items that I know have worked well for me over the years are:

- Calendar

- Training Journal (Notebook)

- Training Dummy

With these three you can do really well, and really boost how you perform at the academy as well as speed the growth process. Let's look at the value of each individually.

CALENDAR

Using a simple desktop calendar to track progress is a very simple and effective visual motivator. I use a blotter style calendar on my desk, it's right beside me as I'm writing this. If you use one of the calendars that you can hang in the kitchen or bathroom then check off the dates as you train so it shows you at a glance how much time you are putting into your jiu jitsu.

As I've mentioned earlier, the aptitude to add time on the mat is the biggest factor in improving your jiu jitsu, but make sure that you are periodizing your training. If you train too hard for 30 days then it's only a matter of time before the injury management section of this manual will come in real handy.

Listen to your body. Even if you feel fit and strong and ready to go, then still mix light workouts, rest days along with hard workouts.

At the white belt level it should be more about learning the techniques and allowing your body to adapt to the style of training that BJJ imposes. There is nothing like specific training or live sparring when it comes to a cardio workout or physical challenge. Many of my training partners and myself have sampled different types of training in an attempt to bolster our training on the mat: CrossFit, Weight Training, Hill Sprints, Fartlek training and much more...but nothing beats live training with a partner who is resisting 50-100%.

Be smart. Log your training days in a visual way and make sure there are some blank spaces in there.

Another method of monitoring your progress is an idea I have stolen from Jerry Seinfeld - 'Don't Break the Chain'. He came up with a system of tracking his progress for writing comedy much like what we discussed above. He used a calendar with no dates just numbered boxes from 1 to 365. As he wrote new sketches each day he would put an X in the box, then the next day he would do the same. This continued until a commitment or some other problem broke the chain of X's. He tried to not break the chain of X's.

He discussed this method with a writing school and told them that his creative output and quality improved so long as he didn't break the chain - a habit formed. Once the chain breaks, you need to get another X back in the box as soon as possible. It's an interesting concept and one I support. For more information on Don't Break the Chain, check this link out: http://lifehacker.com/281626/jerry-seinfelds-productivity-secret

NOTEBOOK NOTES

Keeping a track of your progress is paramount if you are to improve in your jiu jitsu training. My professor recommends that if you improve by only 1% each day then the compounding effect will make you highly proficient in no time.

I have been keeping a training log for many years now and write down my efforts in the class just before I get into bed, this a little routine that now makes for interesting reading years later. I laugh at some of my goals and ambitions as a white and blue belt and laugh even more at some of the complex techniques I thought I might be able to manage - no kidding, there's a flying triangle in there.

Keeping a series of techniques in your head is a complex matter. This is human chess, for every attack there is a defense, for every sweep, takedown, pass, submission there is a counter and counter to that counter. It makes much more sense to keep taking notes than trying to remember what you did. Also, when you review (as you should periodically), some techniques you will identify as being easy to perform and fit your body-type. These techniques I put a star in the corner of the page and come back to drill some more. Then the techniques that present a challenge I put an X in the corner of the page, meaning I need to revisit the move and try and work out what detail I am missing that is making it so hard. The neutral techniques that I don't have a feeling of either way then I let them slide until I come back to them. These are my so-so techniques, I can do them but they don't fill me with joy.

This art form is a process and systems driven. One thing leads logically to another. It's the same position-transition-submission. Simple, right?

The logic though is lightning in a bottle. It needs to be grasped and placed into the correct place in the puzzle or the puzzle cannot be unlocked. Remember how a move was working really well and you were catching everyone or passing everyone, then a couple of weeks later it stopped working? What happened?? Probably, a detail you were applying has now been forgotten, wouldn't it be great if you could go back and retrieve the detail. You can. It's in your training log.

Here's the cycle I discipline myself to implement:

Visualize - This is usually a demo from the coach or professor, or DVD or whatever. Then I see myself doing it, from my own perspective.

Practice - Try the technique out with a partner or grappling dummy. Go through the steps in meticulous detail.

Drill - If it works and 'no parts are missing' then I drill it up to 50-60 times.

Live Training / Test - Once it's working I push myself into a sparring or specific training situation where I can test it. Usually the first couple of times out the gate it fails. Then it clicks and I test it as much as I can.

At the practice stage it enters the training log including the details that made it work so I can move to the drilling stage. If it doesn't work at the drilling stage, go back to Practice and get the training journal out.

Sparring goes in the journal too. I don't spar without a goal in mind, so it's like a convoluted specific training. Convoluted in that, say my goal is back attacks, then I have to go through the process of getting to the back before I can even begin to work my game.

Each element is important and should not be excluded. Once something works well in my game, I go back to cycle one - Visualize.

Here are some of the benefits of using a training journal:

Memory - It's hard to remember all the techniques that you will be picking up in BJJ. This is a sport that is almost completely technique driven, yes, athleticism is a factor but you need the techniques regardless of your athletic prowess. At first the techniques can be a little overwhelming, but then you get the hang of it. As you move to more advanced techniques, again, it becomes a real battle of wits. Your journal is your memory backup. You drop your computer or spill coffee on it and the long-term data is a problem. With your journal or training log, you can drop it and then drop coffee all over and your jiu jitsu brain is safe.

Review - Goal setting is <u>not</u> one of my favorite things, I'm not a big goal guy. I think this may be my aversion to the word and not necessarily what it means. You see, I feel it is imperative to have a point of focus for each session. In the early stages your professor and coach will provide this but as time wears on you'll need to motivate yourself to select techniques that fit your age, physical condition, body shape, weight, and many other factors. This is where you need to start getting creative.

Now if you set the focus of your training you need to check in and see how far along you've come. You can't just reminisce; it's got to be more solid than that. You need review sections in your training log that checks-in and keeps score. How's that half guard sweep coming along? You said you would have it mastered a month ago? Things like this accelerate your progress.

Trackback - Tracing your steps can be an important part of moving forward, especially if you are hitting a plateau. This re-visiting of your previous techniques and the times when your game felt really good can be a reminder that this could happen again in the future. Hitting a plateau can be very disheartening, a real slump pushed me to question whether to continue or not. Using my journal I decided to go back to basics and forget all the fancy techniques that were confusing me. This saved my BJJ career.

Here are some guidelines to keeping a good journal:

- Use symbols and marks that mean something to you. In the Zen Jiu Jitsu Training Log there is a box at the head of the page. This is for you to add a star or check mark or cross to indicate this page is important in some way. That's the way I use the box, you might do something different. You might be creative enough to color the box a shade that reminds you how that training session went.

- Use shorthand when recording your session. For example if you are working a submission from the closed guard, just write 'CG sub'. It makes the whole system easier to manage. No one wants to write an essay after a tough workout.

- Make sure you get into a routine of adding the entries. Like I mentioned earlier I make sure I update the Training Log before I get into bed - on the night I trained. I don't try and remember the next day what I got up to. I try and write it down while it's fresh in my mind. You need to find a routine that works. One of the guys at my school gets his notebook out before he leaves the academy. It's covered in sweat that makes the ink blotchy. That's another tip: Use a pencil, I use a mechanical pencil and it works great, I do use the erasing department too.

- Keep a track on time. In the Zen Training Log we added a start and finish time. This records the overall time you committed to the class. But it also records when you had that class too, Wednesday evening from seven until nine. Great. And if you notice a pattern of stars in the box at the head of the page, then you might find that this is an optimal training time for you.

- Date the entries.

- I know this is repeating myself but it's important. Make sure each class has a goal or focus. Doesn't matter if it was set by the coach or professor or by you. Just make sure there is a focus and you're not just rolling around for the sake of it.

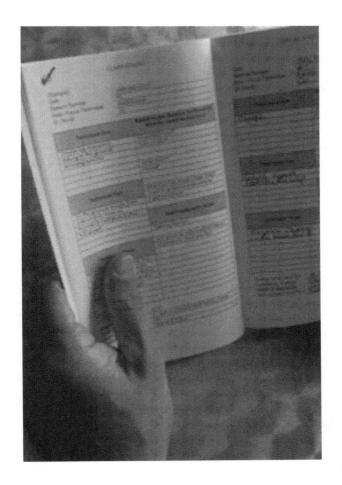

TRAINING DUMMY

THE TRAINING DUMMY - AN EXCERPT FROM THE ZEN JIU JITSU PROGRAM

Please Note: This is not a plug for this or any other dummy. I have no links to this product nor do I receive any compensation for discussing this product here. In fact I don't get any form of sponsorship from any products discussed within this manual. Want to make that clear as it has been mentioned in the past that I'm on the payroll somewhere!?

What if you don't have an academy to train at? Also, what if you train at a school but it's hard to make it every night of the week without divorce papers being filed. The easiest and in my opinion one of the most effective ways to drill is with a training dummy.

Training without a partner is still an excellent way to train. It's virtually impossible to train and have your partner available at all times, plus with a dummy your injury rate reduces dramatically. You can rep techniques and drill your A-moves concentrating on all the small details that make a difference. Even if you only have five or ten minutes spare, with a dummy you can drill for a short time and still feel an improvement.

There are many training dummies out there and I am not going to favor one over the other as I have not trained with them all. It's important that you can train effectively with a dummy and you can afford it. This is the criterion I used when selecting my own:

- Needs to be able to sit up so that closed guard drills work: armbars, omoplatas, triangles, etc.

- Keeps its legs up as a guard defense to practice guard passes.

- Returns its arms back to position so that you don't have to reset it after every rep.

- Keeps its posture in turtle position to practice back techniques, north/south and spinning to back.

- Has a reasonable weight-ratio to simulate a real opponent.

- Knees are positioned up so that stacking drills still work.

My dummy is so important to me that if I moved from one country to another I would make sure that I imported 'Burt' (that's what I call my dummy) with me. My personal choice was the Submission Master. This is not an inexpensive purchase but I believe it is the Rolls Royce of submission dummies.

You may think that a submission dummy is a huge investment and it's true that most dummies are not cheap, but when I compare Jiu Jitsu to most sports it's a pretty reasonable expense. Think about if you wanted to be a really good cyclist - the cost of a good bike? Say you wanted to be good at tennis or golf. Even if we take equipment off the table (which in golf terms is substantial) then the dues at the local tennis or golf clubs would make most BJJ players burst into tears. We get a great service from our academies for a pretty reasonable cost, adding to your tool kit is just a wise choice. I guarantee it.

The only time I see buying a dummy to be a waste is if it never gets used. Make sure when you decide to get a serious drilling aid like this that you build into your program time to drill with the dummy. What you should do is aim for one night per week (at least) maybe when going to the academy doesn't suit your schedule and add that night in for 'Burt' night. Take you laptop or iPad into the garage, spare room or wherever you store him and drill those techniques you've been struggling with. Keep the drilling format the same - the first five minutes should be your A-game submission or sweep and then when you're warm start using the visuals on YouTube, iPad or DVD's to practice. Not many real training partners will be this accommodating? Burt will.

When I first started using a dummy and drilling as I've described above I was accused of all kinds of nefarious activities. I kept Burt under wraps mainly due to embarrassment than anything else, I didn't want the guys to know I had a dummy. I'm pretty sure it would have been easier to admit taking steroids - which was one of the many accusations for the rapid improvement in my technique. My game went from zero to hero using the dummy and staying with the thirty-day Zen program. At this time the thirty day program was just an idea and I had not formulated it as a system or measured its effectiveness. The dummy still paid off though as I started to make ground on guys who I was always level with or slightly worse than. Those guys I can make real progress on now and not worry about getting smashed. It's just 'Jiu Jitsu with Dummies'.

Can you imagine a boxer training without a heavy bag? What if a boxer turned to his coach and said, 'Sorry boss, not hitting the heavy bag tonight, seems like it might give me an advantage over my opponent.' Sure you'll agree this boxer would sound a bit punch drunk? So why do we look down on grappling dummies so much. I think this ties back to drilling. We never drill enough even though all the evidence points to the fact that drilling creates champions. The problem is that rolling is just a ton of fun. There is no getting away from the fact that Jiu Jitsu provides such a fun process of improvement due to the sparring aspect of the overall sport.

Still, boxers spar, boxers hit the bag and speedball because if they spent all their time sparring then they would be wondering where they were and what day it was by the time they hit their forties. Jiu Jitsu is much more forgiving in this aspect so we roll, but that's not where the gold is. We need to drill effectively with or without a partner.

No one bats an eyelid that we use training aids in the strength and conditioning portion of our training to keep your game sharp. Let the gym membership go for a couple of months and grab a more productive tool.

As a warning make sure you don't purchase a throwing dummy thinking it will do and it's cheap. Chances are it won't do the job at all (don't try to knock nails in wood with a pair of pliers, that's the wrong tool for the job) and you will have thrown your money down the drain. Your dummy needs to be Gi friendly and fit the bill outlined at the beginning of this section. When I say Gi friendly I mean a Gi needs to fit onto it so that you can still practice your grips. If you are more Tenth Planet than Nova Uniao then don't worry about the Gi so much but still make sure a rash-guard will fit your dummy. Nothing worse than sweating all over a four hundred dollar investment and finding out there's no way to clean it! They tend not to fit in washing machines.

A grappling dummy is an excellent aid in your development. There is no other method of training - human or otherwise that can let you hit one hundred techniques in fifteen minutes. And you can include that as a cardio workout!

FAQ's from the Submission Master Website on a Grappling Dummy by Bob Dorris

As you may know, Bob sells the Submission Master grappling dummy. This is the dummy that I have but I have no affiliation with Bob and receive no commissions or remuneration in any way for suggesting his products. Please check different dummies out for yourself something new might be on the market that is just as effective. Read what Bob has to say though as the logic is good and applies to any dummy purchase, over to you Bob:

I'm always getting questions from readers about grappling dummy training, so I thought I'd share the Top 3 most frequently asked questions and my responses here with you.

FAQ #1 What is the main purpose of a grappling dummy?

For getting HIGH REPETITIONS WITHOUT A PARTNER. That's it. End of story. Repetitions create muscle memory. Muscle memory allows you to do movements (techniques) quickly and in a coordinated way without having to consciously think about the action. Of all the things you can do to improve your skill, creating muscle memory is undoubtedly the #1 thing you should focus on.

I like to say repetitions are like "rolling a marble through the dirt..." The more times you roll the marble the same way, the deeper the groove in the dirt becomes and the EASIER, FASTER and more EXACT the marble rolls down that path. Reps create a "groove" in your nervous system, causing your techniques to come out "easier, faster and more exact" each time. And, just like riding a bike, you learn them so well it's hard to forget them.

FAQ #2 Why train with a grappling dummy at all? Why not just a live partner?

Although training partners are important for specific techniques and for "rolling", they aren't the most effective way to get high reps of many techniques. Here are 5 good reasons why...

1. You can only train when your partners are available. Grappling dummies are available 24/7. You can even get some decent reps when you have just 5 minutes spare time.

2. Partners can bring your training down to "slow motion". Partners want to talk about the techniques, "the fights on TV", etc. that's not the most effective use of your time and decreases the number of reps you get during your training session.

3.   Partners have to do their reps. Right off the bat, this means you get only half the number of reps that you would if you were training on the grappling dummy.

4.   The more reps your partner does on you, the more abuse to your joints. What do you think is the main reason people stop training? Injuries. It's a no brainer.

5.   When was the last time your training partner let you do 50 triangle chokes on him, followed by 50 heel hooks, then 50 arm bars? Nuff said!

FAQ #3 Is training "in class" enough?

Have you ever taken music lessons? You had to have an instrument at home and practice between lessons, didn't you? And you couldn't practice just when you had someone over to practice with... otherwise it would have taken forever to get good. When you think of it like that, you really can't expect to become very good if you only practice in class, can you? It's only common sense. And a grappling dummy is your "instrument" that allows you to practice between lessons. It's like a boxer having a punching bag to train on in between sparring sessions.

© IMAGE COURTESY OF WWW.GRAPPLINGDUMMY.NET

SPARRING

Here are some tips on Sparring that I think you will find useful:

- Use Observation and monitoring. Size up your opponent before you engage - Use the Observation Strategies outlined earlier. If he makes grips first then you know he is an Attacking player. If he waits for you to get your grips in place then you know he is a Defensive or Counter-Attacking player and will more than likely pull you into his guard.

- Find out what technique your opponent is good at by offering a fake. If your opponent pulls half guard or some other defensive play for a sweep then you know he will want to stay on bottom, he is a guard player. If you fall into a guard position with a view to coming up but your opponent comes on top, then he probably has a top passing game and will look to make side control as soon as he can.

- Try to get your opponent to attack first, either by a fake or just waiting, which frustrates most players. You will quickly learn what technique your opponent relies on, (every player has a favorite technique) then plan a counter for that attack.

- Do not telegraph your attack. Keep it hidden until the last minute.

- Never show wariness when sparring. Play with your game, feel confident. Your opponent will sense if you are wary and go on the attack, however, the image of a low gas tank and uncertainty in attacks can be used as a fake.

- When you and your opponent are close make sure your base is solid. Never be flat on your back always look for angles.

- Always set up your opponent before you sweep. Set up your grips and base then sweep. Don't go early and try to use muscle. Most experienced fighters will never let you sweep them unless you set them up.

- Always relax your body before you sweep. Tension slows down the movement of the hip. Visualize a snake attacking its prey. Uses its hips to move. Calm, relaxed, then BAM, lightening speed.

- Close the gap between your thought and action. Don't think too long or the opportunity will fade. Go for it when the timing feels right. This is sparring, not the World Champs, now is the time to take risks.

- The moment to set up an attack is when he is about to launch an attack or as he is settling into his base after an attack.

- Always remember when your opponent attacks part of their balance will usually be exposed for a counter attack or sweep. This applies to your counter as well, keep that mind.

- If you are constantly clashing with your opponent then you must work on timing.

- Focus on the technique in your mind without looking at your opponent as a person. Just play the technique out. Your opponent is actually you.

- Don't try a sweep to be just sweeping. Don't try and arm bar just for the sake of trying it. Make each technique have a purpose in the context of the roll.

- Don't feel the need to spend time on escapes when there is no danger. If it doesn't feel like you are threatened maintain an attacking position.

- Pace your energy. No one has an infinite gas tank and muscle sweeps burn up energy like nothing else. Burst. Rest. Burst. Rest.

- If your opponent has a great bottom game, pull guard first. If he has a great top game try and pass.

- If your game is not working disengage. Take the time to go back to Step 1: Observe, what are you missing?

- Watch your opponents balance and base. Is he solid or does he look off balance, if so isolate his posting arm and sweep to that side. Sometimes it's as easy as a simple pushing action.

- Use lapels to wrap arms. If he only has three limbs at his disposal you are in a greater advantageous position.

- Never offer your back unless you have a killer turtle escape.

- Don't try to score with the first sweep. Statistically you need to score first to win, but the first attack doesn't have to be the scoring move. Have your mind in position to attack number two and number three.

- The most common position used in BJJ is the half guard. Learn various escapes and counters, including if your head is controlled or if you have the top position and need to get out of it.

- When all else fails have a guard position that you can rely on. Default back to that guard regardless of what happens - this is your reset.

- Every attack has a counter, don't forget this is human chess. Learn the counters.

- If you get swept or submitted never lose your cool and go after your opponent. This just creates more openings for counters and you will probably get subbed.

- When up against a counter attacker, offer plenty of fake attacking opportunities. This will expose his game, allowing you to attack.

- Control the space. Always.

- Don't try that flying arm bar triangle combo when sparring unless you are really high level, then it's okay.

- If you get caught with a counter disengage and re-group right away. Don't wait for the sub before you come back to the game.

- When you decide to attack for the submission there should be no doubt or hesitation. You need to commit, or the counter is wide open.

- Sometimes it's wise to just defend early in the game, especially if your opponent is much bigger. Keep a good guard, roll to turtle if you can, escape and make them move. Once they begin to tire start to work your game.

- Attacking is as exhausting as defending.

- Never underestimate any of your opponents, and never underestimate your own abilities.

- No two opponents are the same. Nullify his defense and exploit his weakness.

- Sparring has three phases of energy: Release Energy, Reserve Energy and Regeneration Energy.

MAPS AND SYSTEMS

PULLING IT ALL TOGETHER

At a recent seminar with Caio Terra a question was asked in the Q&A section, which was enlightening. "Do you have a game plan as soon as you step onto the mat in a competition?"

Caio smiled, laughed a little, "No. That wouldn't make sense. If I had a pre-defined game plan and my opponent moved away from that game plan then I would be screwed. The techniques have to be responsive due to the amount of time I spent preparing and training, I then react to whatever my opponent does. This strategy works best."

This is a very interesting idea and also tells us that Caio is a counter-attacking fighter. Every fighter needs to counter attack at some point so having counters is a very high level concept. While in the white belt phase this is a good habit to attain but can also lead to frustration if neither training partner is willing to commit to anything.

Following are a series of chain-link systems that can help a white belt get into better positions. I've structured the "Maps" from the perspective of a position. This will give you a decent starting point with regard to what you should do next should you arrive in this position. Don't forget, this manual is not expansive enough to cover every eventuality and will not cover the transition to a dominant position; this can only develop as your game develops. Once you can survive for a period of time without getting submitted by a higher-ranking belt then you will need to start to move into better positions and this map system will help.

You may not be totally familiar with all the techniques outlined. Use the Internet, YouTube or the Resources section at the back of this manual to help with clarity. Don't forget to seek advice from your professor and coaches.

I use the expression chain-link because one thing links to the next as you will see in the tables below:

Closed Guard Bottom (Attacking)
Series One
Cross Grips (your right hand in your opponents right collar across)
Armbar attack
  Armbar defended
Armbar to Triangle
  Triangle Defended
Flower Sweep to Mount

Series Two
Cross Grips
X Choke (Palms up/down)
  Choke defended
Hip Bump (Sit Up) Sweep to Mount
  Hip Bump Blocked with Base
Kimura
  Kimura Defended
Reverse Armbar

Series Three
Cross Grips
Opponent Stands to Break Guard
Ankle Sweep to Mount

Side Control Top (Attacking)
Series One
Control Hips Blocked
Keylock
  Keylock defended
Spinning Armbar
  Armbar defended
Move back to North South Choke

Series Two
Control Hips Blocked
Move up to Knee on Belly
  Knee on Belly defended
Spinning Armbar

Series Three
Control Hips Blocked
Knee on Belly
   Knee on Belly defended
Remove defense move to Mount

Mount Top (Attacking)
Series One
Low mount, position stabilized
X-Choke
   Defended by Upa
Trap Arm to S-Mount Armbar

Series Two
High Mount, position stabilized
Keylock
   Keylock defended
Trap Arm to S-Mount Armbar
   Armbar defended
Armbar Switch

Back Mount Attacking
Series One
Back Control, position stabilized, shoulders level
Rear Naked Choke
   RNC Defended
Bow and Arrow Choke

Series Two
Back Control, position stabilized, shoulders not-level, opponent scooted down
   Basic lapel choke (get reaction)
      Lapel defended
   Armbar from Back

Series Three
Turtle Control
   Escape Attempt

Clock choke

Combination Drills
Armbar - Triangle - Omoplata from Closed Guard
Armbar - Triangle - Armbar from Closed Guard
Cross Knee Pass to Cross Collar Choke
Sit Up Sweep - Triangle - Omoplata
X-Choke - Armbar - Switch Armbar from Closed Guard
Flower Sweep - Triangle - Omoplata
From Back Mount - Lapel Choke - Bow and Arrow - Armbar

IN CONCLUSION

"Transcend the realm of life and death, and then you will be able to make your way calmly and safely through any crisis that confronts you."
~ Morihei Ueshiba - Father of Aikido

Like I said at the beginning of this manual, I am envious of your position as a white belt. Your next color is blue and this is again a significant step along your pathway in jiu jitsu. As you progress your confidence level will increase too, you will begin to feel more like a jiu jitsu fighter than just a guy or a girl doing jiu jitsu for the first time. As the stripes on your white belt start to mount and the techniques that were once as strange as anything you've ever known become somewhat familiar then you will know what an amazing sport this is.

White belts so very often only get so far then find some reason to stop. Don't let this be you. Just remember 'every black belt you see started once right where you are'. You're a black belt ... you just don't know it yet.

If you have enjoyed this book then go back to the beginning and re-read it (also leave a review if you have time), or just dip into sections that we covered that piqued your interest, especially the Core Principles. I hope you enjoyed this journey as much I did putting it together. It was an education for me too. If you have any comments, additions or ideas, please get in touch via my website at:
http://jiujitsubuddha.com
I would love to hear from you and your thoughts on the concepts and ideas discussed. Maybe we'll meet on the mat some day, I very much look forward to it.
Be water, my friend.

RESOURCES AND REFERENCE

REFERENCES:
University of Jiu Jitsu. Saulo Ribeiro and Kevin Howell. Victory Belt Publishing 2008
Outliers. Malcolm Gladwell. Back Bay Books 2011
Roadmap to the Zone. Robert S Neff Ph.d. And Michael K Garza Ed.D. Authorhouse 2004
2012 World Jiu Jitsu Championships Case Study. BishopBjj.com
The Essence of Buddhism. David Tuffley. Kindle Edition 2011
Joe Lewis Fighting Systems

RECOMMENDED READING:
University of Jiu Jitsu. Saulo Ribeiro and Kevin Howell. Victory Belt Publishing 2008
Roadmap to the Zone. Robert S Neff Ph.d. And Michael K Garza Ed.D. Authorhouse 2004
Jiu Jitsu Unleashed. Eddie Bravo. McGraw-Hill 2005
The X Guard. Marcelo Garcia with Eric Krauss and Glen Cordoza. Victory Belt Publishing 2008.
The Cauliflower Chronicles. Marshal D Carper. Victory Belt Publishing 2010

RECOMMENDED WATCHING:
Jeff Glovers Deep Half Guard. Cryo Productions 2009
Saulo Ribeiro Jiu Jitsu Revolution. Series 1 and 2.
Robson Moura. Fusion 1 and 2.
111 Half Guard Techniques with Caio Terra. Cryo Productions 2011
Caio Terra Modern Jiu Jitsu. Mobile Black Belt 2012
Fight Club. 20th Century Fox. 2002.

RECOMMENDED WEBSITES:
http://bjjtech.com/tech/
http://bishopbjj.com

http://fightlogmedia.com
http://www.igrapple.com
http://www.grapplingdummy.net
http://armbarsoap.com
http://youtu.be/CWgke2m__6Y
http://youtu.be/4JsEOI5sLRM
http://youtu.be/KilhUNQ6r7U
http://www.joelewisfightingsystems.com
http://tapordiecompany.com

Three of my favorites:
Grapplers Guide 2.0
http://www.grapplersguide.com
Mendes Bros Online Training Program
http://www.mendesbros.com
Marcelo Garcia in Action
https://www.mginaction.com/default.aspx

TRAINING AIDS

Zen Jiu Jitsu Training Log on Amazon -
http://www.amazon.com/gp/product/1482667665

Grappling Dummies:
http://www.grapplingdummy.net
http://www.grapplingdummy.com

Made in the USA
Middletown, DE
25 March 2023